The Tandem Scoop
An Insider's Guide to Tandem Cycling
by John Schubert

BURLEY DESIGN COOPERATIVE
Eugene, Oregon USA

ISBN 0-9637190-0-9

Published and distributed by:
    Burley Design Cooperative
    4080 Stewart Road
    Eugene, OR 97402 USA
    (503) 687-1644

Printed and bound in the United States of America
96 95 94 93   5 4 3 2 1

 Printed on Recycled Paper with Soy-Based Inks

Mixte X is a trademark of Burley Design Cooperative.
Uptube is a trademark of Richard Jorgensen.

Foreword

Here's a book about tandems and tandeming. It is for people who are considering a tandem purchase, and for tandem owners—both new and experienced.

Single (or solo) bike information is plentiful. Many cyclists already know all about how to ride, how to enjoy riding, and how to cope with flat tires or headset repairs. Others are happy to be mechanically disinclined, and instead visit their local bike shop for service. Tandems, however, offer a whole new set of variables. Tandemists need to know why tandems get flats and wear out headsets so often. In addition to technical information they want a resource book that discusses elusive subjects like what to look for when buying a tandem, how to make sure they enjoy their tandem, techniques for the captain and stoker, and tips for tandem teamwork (things that are neither obvious nor applicable from single bike experience).

Subjects like derailleur adjustment and wheel truing have been left out of this book because they are universal, and there are numerous good books and magazines available that deal with general bicycle repair and design. Instead, each of the following chapters discusses a subject peculiar to tandems.

As the first book of its type (that we know of), it's inevitable that *The Tandem Scoop* will be incomplete,

and certain subjects will be debated. The tandem market is small but very diverse. Several opinions often exist on any one subject. It is beyond our scope to reconcile those opinions or offer the definitive tandem guide, if such a thing could exist.

Our aim is to present straightforward, proven techniques, advice, and technical information. When varying opinions exist we try to point out the strengths and weaknesses of all viewpoints. We also try to convey just how fun tandeming is.

As a leading supplier of tandems we have resisted almost every temptation to promote Burley tandems throughout this book. By providing a tandem resource book we hope instead to promote tandeming in general.

For those who don't yet know everything there is to know about tandems, read on. We offer you *The Tandem Scoop*.

Bruce Creps
Burley Design Cooperative

Dedication

To the woman who pinches my backside whenever I ride too slowly: Thanks for a million memories. May there be millions more to come.

Contents

Save it kid, those four-legged ones are impossible to catch!

1 • The Thrill of Speed

Fifty-five m.p.h. may seem a bit dull in a car, but on a bicycle it's a gas. It can be an everyday occurrence if you ride your tandem in rolling countryside.

You don't even need a very steep descent. All it takes is a few hundred yards of 10-percent grade—a tad steeper than a freeway ramp—and vvvvvvvrooooommm. You'll match the speed of motorists on the descent, hold 45 m.p.h. through the trough at the bottom, and, if your teamwork is right, maintain 20 m.p.h. or better up the next rise and over the top. On a long, flat stretch, you can cruise at 30 m.p.h. and do frisky sprints at 40 m.p.h.

And you don't have to be a superhuman to do it. These speeds are for ordinary, fun-loving bike riders like you and me.

This, friends, is why I fell in love with tandems and bought one more than a decade ago. The tandem's romantic togetherness is well and good, but to me, that's a minor fringe benefit.

I like to go fast on a machine that feels secure at speed, and a good tandem meets this criterion.

Why so fast? You have twice the horsepower for about the same wind resistance as your single bike. So you go faster. Down hills, the advantage multiplies: the added weight makes you roll faster. (Remember when Galileo dropped the two balls of unequal weights off the Leaning Tower of Pisa? They fell at the same speed, but that demonstration told only half the story. Add a bunch of wind resistance and a small amount of rolling resistance as with a bicycle, and the heavier object goes faster downhill. Your physics teacher can elaborate on this.)

All this extra speed would be a prescription for disaster if the tandem didn't have superior braking and roadholding to match. But it does (on dry pavement).

A good tandem has braking superior to a single bike. What limits the braking on the single bike is the possibility of pitching over the front wheel if you brake too hard. On the tandem, though, you have a friend's weight to help hold the rear wheel to the pavement.

Moreover, the extra weight means that the tandem isn't jostled by bumps the way a single bike is. It plows through them; the weight of two people pushing the tires down helps maintain more secure contact with the road. On bumpy pavement, a tandem can pull away from single road bikes simply because of its better roadholding. The tires and front forks do more to cushion your ride than they do on a single bike.

When I want to demonstrate to curious riders what a tandem can do, I take them on a four-mile course that includes a dirt road, steep bumpy descents, steep smooth descents, shallow twisting descents, and, well, some climbing to make up for all those descents. Several people have decided to buy a tandem for themselves after that short ride.

The dirt road and bumpy pavement show the bike's roadholding abilities. On the first descent, I demonstrate the tandem's superior braking, so my new stoker won't be worried about how fast we get going later in the ride. I let the bike coast up to about 20 m.p.h.

"Okay, I'm going to show you how good the brakes are," I say. "Hang on tight." I then squeeze the cantilever brakes hard and slow the bike to walking speed.

Every time I make this demonstration, my new stoker is amazed. No one has ever felt a bike slow down so abruptly.

We speed up to 45 or so on a bumpy descent. The bike feels much more secure than a single bike. The tandem seems to slice through the bumps; a single is tossed about like a rowboat on high seas on that particular road.

Soon, we reach a smooth-but-twisty country road which descends at a shallow three percent. Most cars go 30 on that stretch. We go 35 and feel very much in control as we pass the cars. Finally, we reach a smooth, steep descent with a well-banked curve at the bottom. Leaning through that curve at top speed, we frequently sprint to pass cars on the following straightaway.

Fast? You bet. But what makes it fun for the new stoker is how stable and secure the bike feels, no matter what the speed or the pavement surface underneath.

Okay, I'm going to show you how good the brakes are!

The four-mile ride is only a teaser, of course. We frequently take the tandem on day-long rides and week-long tours. We never tire of its superior speed and handling.

In both formal and informal competition, tandems are often used to win century and double-century events. Eight-hour double centuries are not uncommon, and mere mortals can ride them in ten hours. (Chapter 10 gives the lowdown on tandem stage racing, a long-overdue variant of the world's greatest sport.)

So, what is it like to cruise all afternoon at 27 m.p.h. on 20 m.p.h. legs (or at 22 m.p.h. on 16 m.p.h. legs)? It's wonderful! The presence of another rider on the same bicycle helps you keep your rhythm up. Teamwork brings out the best in both of you, and you can enjoy greater synergy than even the best pair of riders on single bikes.

The tandem is a more efficient machine, so it goes faster. It is a teamwork machine, so two riders can enjoy working together with a closeness unmatched by any other sport.

And someday, your stoker will poke you in the ribs with delight—because you just passed a Porsche (well, okay, maybe a Mustang) on a twisty road. The outdoor life doesn't ever get any better than that.

Editor's note: John Schubert gleefully describes the thrill of speed from his perspective as a confident, experienced cyclist. Although speed can be thrilling, we need to remind you that bicycling, like most sports, involves a certain amount of risk. Even on a tandem, things like passing cars, going 45 m.p.h. on a bumpy descent, and high speed in general increase the risk of accident and injury, and should only be done by highly experienced cyclists using good judgement on safe roads. Don't push the speed envelope until you've ridden enough to be an expert at controlling the tandem, and don't ever ride too fast for the sight distances on your road. Scan vigilantly for potholes and the like. Going fast is lots of fun, but it isn't playing.

2 • The Fun of Togetherness

Lots of times, I see people going for a ride "together" on their single bikes. Slight differences in ability keep them separated by 100 yards or more. If they ride together in paceline formation, they'll be closer together; but the rider in the back has to watch the front rider so closely that s/he can't see much of the scenery.

A tandem takes care of all these problems. The riders are about two feet away from each other, so they can speak in a normal tone of voice. What a change from riding single bikes! Never will a hill or a traffic signal interrupt your conversation.

For friends or spouses whose time together is limited, a tandem adds an important dimension to cycling: while you're enjoying all the benefits of a bike ride, you remain close together so you can converse, enjoy silent shared time, and share the experiences of cycling more closely than riders on single bikes.

People unfamiliar with tandeming often assume the person in the back seat is getting a raw deal. "It's like being a sled dog," I've heard people say. "Only the lead dog gets a change of scenery." They also complain that the controls are all in front. For the average tandem team (husband in front, wife in back), the arrangement may appear chauvinistic.

Oh, but riding in the back has substantial hidden advantages. (For the record, I do drive a dogsled in the winter, and the "stoker" dogs love it.) The stoker has a much better view than the captain. Sure, s/he can't see straight ahead without craning the neck some, but the view to the sides is excellent—like the view out of a train window. Because the stoker doesn't have to steer or watch for road hazards, s/he is free to watch the scenery full time. It makes for a lot of fun riding.

Stoking is also warmer on cold days—the captain's body shelters you from the wind. Also, you don't get mud in your face when riding in the rain, as you would on a single bike.

Should the stoker share the captain's work load by having some of the controls? Some tandem teams prefer that.

My wife and I tried to share the work by putting the controls to our third (drum) brake on the rear handlebars, but found we didn't like that arrangement. She couldn't see when to brake and needed me to tell her. This "verbal linkage" made the reaction time too slow.

Some of our friends have set up their bikes with the shift levers in the back. That wouldn't work very well for us, but they like it. We have now settled on a different approach: instead of shift levers, the stoker gets a small camera, tucked in the captain's jersey pocket. The stoker's job is to take good pictures while the bike rolls— and we have some beautiful ones from our vacations in Vermont. (This doesn't end with the camera; my wife keeps compact binoculars and a map in my other jersey pockets.)

I'm reluctant to preach too much about teamwork on a bicycle or in a marriage, because I get tired of hearing such preaching from others. But the teamwork of riding together on a tandem can form a powerful bond between two people. When you've worked together to get through a mountain pass, and shared the reward of the breathtaking view at the top, you feel a closeness that defies explanation.

3 • How to Select a Tandem

If you've read this far, the hook is set nicely. If you don't own one, you're thinking of getting a tandem. Now some questions arise: How do I choose? Which one is the best value?

To start with, you can't use most of the yardsticks you would use to buy a good single bike. With single bikes, frames tend to be very similar from one company to the next, and they blur into the background. Many buyers look for the component group they want and buy the cheapest bike that has that group.

That won't work on a tandem. Tandem components tend to be a mix of items that meet the tandemist's needs for durability and performance. Tandem frames do differ from one another, much more

See Jan, these bikes here are more expensive because they're "double-butted"!

Figure 3.1

Parts of a Tandem

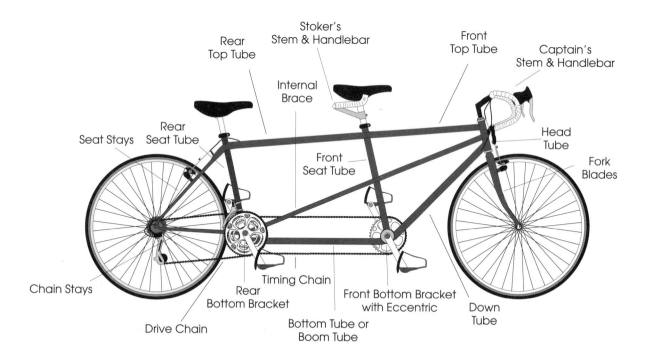

than single bike frames. And the overall package differs more than with most single bikes, because different makers have different ideas about how to please two riders at once. Some tandems are racing oriented, some touring oriented, some husband-and-wife oriented, and some are, well, hard to figure out.

Here are some things your tandem frame needs to have:

Correct Steering Geometry

A tandem isn't a single bike, and its steering geometry must be different. If the front of a tandem is designed like a single, it will steer like a truck. It will be very difficult and fatiguing to handle, and you'll get tired wrestling with it. The key difference is in a dimension called "trail" (see Figure 3.2). Trail confers high-speed stability and makes a bike steer in the direction that it's leaned in (and it's the reason you can ride a single bike no-hands). Since a tandem has a stoker leaning independently of the captain, you want less trail. A tandem with too much trail fights you. At low speeds trail creates wheel flop,

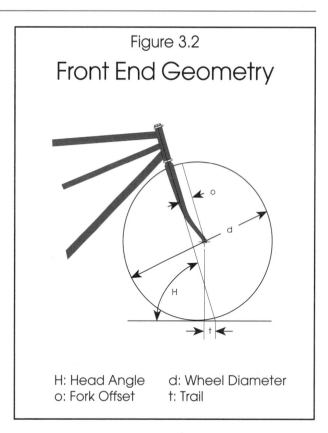

Figure 3.2

Front End Geometry

H: Head Angle   d: Wheel Diameter
o: Fork Offset   t: Trail

and because tandems climb slowly (sometimes) and can be hard to control at those times, less trail is also appropriate.

Most single bikes have 2 1/4 inches of trail. Tandems should have approximately 1 3/4 to 1 7/8 inches of trail, which comes from a 73-degree head-tube angle with 2 1/8 inches of fork rake or offset. This specific combination is hard, if not impossible, to improve upon.

Oversize Tubing

A tandem frame is so big that it can sway visibly from one end to another if the frame isn't stiff enough. Oversize tubing helps provide that stiffness. Among good-quality steel tandems, you'll find the steel used is virtually always chrome-moly alloy, which is durable and strong. More expensive tandems often use double-butted tubing (which has a thicker wall at the ends where the tubes are joined, and a thinner section in the middle). All else being equal, a properly designed double-butted frameset will be lighter, without sacrificing performance.

Excellent oversize aluminum frames are available, although they tend to be among the more expensive tandems. Titanium tandems exist, but the price is prohibitive for us mere mortals. Test ride the types that interest you and decide for yourself based on comfort, handling, and stability (as well as price and availability).

The Best Internal Bracing

Generally speaking, tandem frames need bracing for durability and strength. But some bracing designs are ineffective; some just add weight; some give the bike a harsh ride but do little to keep the frame from swaying. And some keep the frame from swaying but also have a harsh ride.

A few builders offer tandems without an internal brace. This design has a bad reputation, because some of the worst, most flexible frames of 20 years ago were built from standard bike tubing in this "open" style. But the best of today's open frames may surprise you. Of course, they aren't as rigid as otherwise-identical frames with internal bracing. But a well-designed open frame

Figure 3.3

Common Tandem Frame Styles

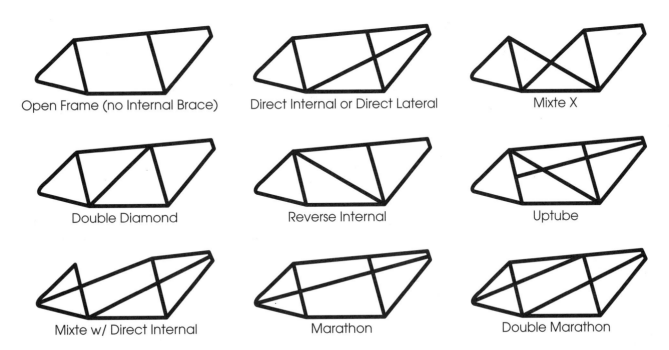

Open Frame (no Internal Brace)   Direct Internal or Direct Lateral   Mixte X

Double Diamond   Reverse Internal   Uptube

Mixte w/ Direct Internal   Marathon   Double Marathon with oversize tubing can meet the needs of a wide variety of riders.

Included among these riders are those who use the tandem for around-town recreation and low-key club rides, including centuries. And an open frame is ideal for use with a childback conversion.

Also included are some racing teams. If you and your racing partner ride together with exceptional smoothness, are skilled bike handlers, and crave weight reduction, this (or the double diamond described below) may be your preferred mount.

I prefer a braced tandem, because I want more frame rigidity under hard cornering. And I think just about all riders would want bracing for loaded touring or serious off-road riding—instances where you need the additional stability.

The most common bracing scheme among tandems sold today is an oversize bracing tube which runs from the head tube to the rear bottom bracket, often referred to as a direct internal or direct lateral. It's a common configuration for good reasons—it provides an excellent combination of stiffness in hard cornering and minimizes the harshness of the ride.

Several other more complicated designs including twin laterals (paired tubes which run from the head tube to the rear dropouts) and the original Jack Taylor "marathon" bracing (a large single tube running from the head tube to the middle of the stoker's seat tube where it joins an extra set of rear stays) have faded from the marketplace because the direct internal does the job well and it's easy to manufacture.

Moreover, most tandems get used for touring and/or a child stoker at some point in their lives; the direct internal is very compatible with these uses. It doesn't get in the way of the stoker conversion hardware, and it leaves lots of places to put water bottles for those long barren stages.

Another effective frame design is the double diamond, so-named because the brace (which runs parallel to the down tube) divides the frame into two diamond-shaped parallelograms when viewed from the side. Some of the first safety tandems of a century ago used this configuration, and the double diamond—along with its

A framebuilder's view of unfinished joints on (A) TIG-welded and (B) fillet-brazed frames. Fillet-brazed joints require more cleanup work and result in seamlessly smooth transitions between the tubes.

modern variant, the reverse internal—are familiar setups nowadays. They're a smidgen less stiff and slightly lighter in weight than the direct internal design—a worthwhile trade-off for many riders.

Is there more than one way to tuna fish? You bet! Some tandem designers achieve extensive rigidity by ovalizing tubes against side-to-side bending. Others use round tubes, placed so they resist torsional stresses. As mentioned above, there are all sorts of different bracing configurations. The possible permutations are endless, and many of them can be made to work quite well. Remember, your riding style and what the tandem is used for are as pertinent to your needs as frame design. A comparative test ride is the best way to find which one is right for you.

Durable, Simple Construction

Tandem frame tubes are usually joined by tungsten inert gas (TIG) welding or fillet brazing. Thanks to mountain bikes, TIG welding has become accepted, respected, and requested because of its strength, durability, and production-line efficiency. Although TIG welding uses higher temperatures than brazing, TIG welding can be carried out quickly, so the heat spreads to a very small portion of the tube (excessive heat can weaken and distort the joints).

Tandem frames are not usually lugged. Lugs, in the small quantities used for oversize tandem frames, would be prohibitively expensive and would limit variations in frame size and geometry. Some framebuilders, notably Tom Kellogg and Bill Boston, have made custom tandems with handmade, custom lugs. You wouldn't like the price for such extensive handwork. Some builders slip-fit tubing over certain joints for reinforcement—something like an exaggerated external-butted tube.

It's important to note that you aren't giving anything up by not having a brazed, lugged frame. Lugs have remained common in single road bikes because they're pretty, and because single road bikes are made in a traditional, old-fashioned way. In most safety-critical metal applications (pressurized nuclear reactor piping, airplane engine mounts, that sort of thing) weld-ing is standard and brazing isn't even allowed. (It's not allowed because welded joints are easier to inspect.)

Fillet-brazed joints are also very strong, although they are more time-consuming to fabricate and finish than TIG-welded ones. As a result, fillet-brazed joints cost more, but for some can be a beautiful and essential part of the bike. The choice boils down to this: do you want to spend, oh, an additional $500 for pretty metalwork?

There are a few poorly made tandems which appear at our nation's garage sales now and again. They look like they were thrown together from standard-size single bike frame tubing, and aren't convincingly braced. These bikes are fun only for the smoothest, gentlest ride. Otherwise, they introduce you to the feel of "stoker lag."

Stoker lag occurs in cornering or quick maneuvers. To the riders, it feels as though the captain turns or straightens out and there is a lag before the stoker does the same. These "wet-noodle frames" are not the sport tandems this book endorses. Tandems which exhibit consid-

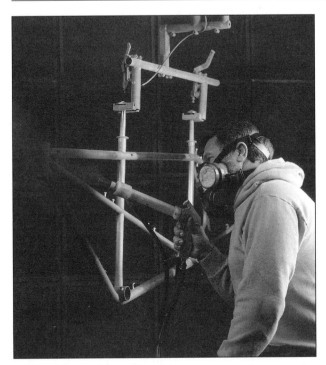

The powder coating process in action. The powder particles are electrically charged and projected at the bike frame as a dry spray.

erable stoker lag can be difficult, if not impossible, to control under the frisky riding conditions I gleefully described earlier. Such tandems can be dangerous if you exceed their modest capabilities, and should be restricted to cruising the boardwalk or other leisurely riding. (It's just as well. These tandems generally have poor components to go with their flexible frames, and component failures are frequent enough that you don't want to be a long walk from home.)

Plentiful Brazed-on Bosses

You'll have two riders' needs to tend to, so you'll want plenty of ways to tend to those needs. A good tandem will have threaded bosses for front and rear racks and fenders, and four water bottles. A pump peg and chain hanger are nice, too.

Great Paint

No matter how much you want to save a buck, you still don't want a paint job that looks cruddy or chips easily.

For those who want a classic finish, sprayed-on polyurethane paints (like Glasurit and duPont's Imron) are an excellent choice. They offer a wide choice of colors and a deep, lustrous shine. However, regulations continue to pile up. Only those painters who can afford special booths and equipment will be able to continue to use these sprayed-on finishes.

Powder coating has come a long way in the past decade. As the name implies, the finish is sprayed on as a dry powder. An electrostatic charge is used to attract the powder to the surface of the electrically grounded frame and to provide uniform wrapping around the frame tubes. The powdered frame is then baked, which melts the coating and creates a smooth, glossy finish. The net result is less expensive, more durable, and environmentally friendlier than sprayed-on, solvent-based paints. And with two-coat processes, powder finishes are starting to look very respectable.

Keep in mind. a tandem repaint can be costly, as in several hundred dollars. Get a quote first if you are purchasing a used tandem that needs repaint. Your local bike shop can probably refer you to a painter who specializes in bicycles.

Space for the Rear Rider

On a tandem, the stoker's handlebar stem faces rearward instead of forward like the stem on the front of the bike. Thus the rear top tube must be much longer than the front top tube to compensate. What are the numbers? Select a rear top tube approximately 27 inches long, and an average height woman will find the reach to the handlebars is about the same as on her proportionally designed single bike.

Early tandems were about 23 inches (or less) in the rear, and stokers found their noses against the captain's back or their knees hitting their elbows. Be warned: if the stoker is cramped and uncomfortable, you won't tandem as far or as often.

You may ask, "Why not make that tube much longer for taller stokers?" Most custom builders will make top tubes out to 26 or 27 inches, but not much beyond that. This is because the stoker doesn't have to steer so s/he can relax the upper body. Without the need for steering, one can be quite comfortable with the bars a few inches closer than on a single bike.

Longer rear top tubes—and I've tried them up to and beyond 30 inches—add to the wheelbase, which can reduce stiffness and detract from handling.

The Right Size for You

Most important: The frame should be none too big for the captain. If in doubt, too small is better than too big. The captain must have straddle clearance over the top tube, because s/he will need to be able to stop the bike and keep it upright while the stoker remains strapped into both pedals. (That's how most good tandemists wait at stop signs and lights; it makes for the quickest getaway.) On mountain tandems make sure the captain's frame size is two to three inches smaller than a road tandem's to allow for higher bottom brackets and additional straddle clearance. (See Chapter 9 for more on this.)

If you're considering a tandem with a sloping top tube (which most tandems have), you've got another reason to buy small. The sloping top tube increases the effective size of the frame, because the head tube is higher than the seat lug where the frame size is measured.

Size matters less for the stoker. The stoker has two concerns: seat position and hand position. Because the stoker can mount and dismount as you would mount a horse or motorcycle (while the captain holds the bike upright), straddle clearance is much less critical. So if need be, the stoker's seat can be low, close to the top tube. At the other extreme, the stoker's seat can go as high as today's ultra-long seat posts want to place it, up in the flagpole-sitting stratosphere. One caveat: if you're planning to spend a lot of your time riding off-road, the stoker should probably have adequate standover clearance to allow for emergency bailouts.

The stoker's hand position is determined by the rear stem and handlebars, and the placement of the rear stem on the captain's seat post. Assuming the captain's seat is not bottomed out, there's no problem to move the handlebars up or down as per your needs. If the limited horizontal movement of the standard stoker stem does not provide enough versatility, you may want to obtain an adjustable stoker stem (see Figure 3.4). Although it weighs an additional half pound, it allows for several inches of fore-aft adjustment of the stoker's handlebars. This can make a world of difference for the short stoker riding on a large-frame bike. In addition, if the stoker wants a choice of riding positions, or you plan to ride with two or more stokers, this option may be for you.

On a single bike, adjusting an off-size frame in this way would screw up the fore-aft weight distribution and result in lousy handling. But this isn't the case on a tandem, because the long wheelbase mitigates these changes. If you can get the seat-to-crank-spindle distance that fits your body, the other factors will fall into place.

Stock sizes on better tandems can comfortably accommodate more than 95 percent of the tandem teams out there. If you're part of the remaining five percent, expect to pay a bit more for a custom fit.

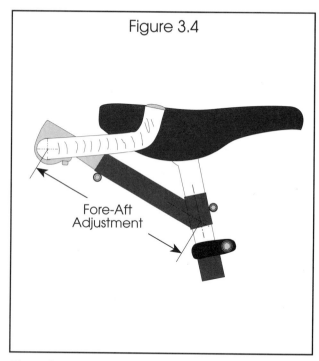

Figure 3.4

Fore-Aft
Adjustment

The adjustable stoker stem allows fine tuning the stoker's position, and gives correct handlebar reach for short adults and child stokers.

A frame that meets all the above criteria needs suitable parts to match. Here are the most important things to look for:

Front Fork

Tandem forks have it rough. They eat a lot of bumps since tandems are less maneuverable than singles. The stresses of riding are amplified by the higher speeds and added weight of a tandem, too.

The front fork bears a significant part of the braking and cornering forces, so tandem forks need extra-beefy blades for stable handling and composed emergency stops. Oversize steerer tubes (1 1/8 or 1 1/4 inch rather than 1 inch in diameter) and corresponding stems and headsets have become quite popular for tandems in recent years. These oversized parts add strength and stiffness to the front end of the bike, thus improving control and reliability. Although much of the current crop of oversize hardware was developed for mountain bikes, this isn't really a new concept—since the turn of the century, top-quality tandems have been built with special parts including jumbo headsets and steerer tubes.

Wide-Range Gearing That Shifts Every Time

Why wide-range, even for tandem teams that plan no loaded touring? Well, tandems occasionally bog down on steep climbs. If one

With its extra horsepower, a tandem requires bigger gears than a single. Pictured here are cranks with an enormous 61-tooth setup (left), and a larger-than-average 54-tooth chainring (right).

rider is tired, or if coordination between riders suffers a momentary lapse, you need low gears to help you regain your momentum.

At the other extreme, the high-speed capabilities of a tandem allow you to spin through gears that would be impossible to pedal on a single. On a fast descent, you can't have too tall a gear on a tandem. Chainrings with 61 teeth and 11-tooth cogs are not unheard of! Experienced tandemists generally get their highs by using large chainrings rather than super-small cogs, because increasing the number of teeth reduces wear and distributes drivetrain forces more evenly.

When you need high gears—or low gears—you need them now. Because the captain is two feet farther away from the derailleurs than on a single, it's harder to get a clean shift. Be sure to select a proven indexed derailleur system with matching chain and freewheel. With a tandem's long cables the 6-speed can be less finicky than the narrower 7- or 8-speed freewheels. The 7-speed is the norm, however, and in most cases works fine.

Wheels That Won't Quit

You'll want strong rims specially made for the greater stresses of tandem use. If you've ever taken a loaded tandem with single bike wheels into a high-speed turn and watched the rims flex—threatening to become potato chips before your very eyes—you will forget about trying to save a few ounces. With the exception of lightweight racing tandem teams, you'll want 48 spokes for tandems with 700C or 27-inch rims.

Recently, some tandem builders started making fast "road tandems" using the lighter, stronger, 26-inch wheels that have evolved from mountain bike singles. The 26-inch wheels will do fine with 36 spokes for all but the heaviest tandem teams or severest abuse.

Brakes

As I said earlier, tandems can outstop singles because you get braking on both wheels and don't have to worry about pitching over the handlebars. Cantilever brakes have improved dramatically in the past few years. The improved brakes give you added ease in controlling this

Magura hydraulic brakes use fluid-filled hoses instead of cables to control braking. Each side of the brake mechanism has a hydraulic cylinder that presses the brake pad against the rim.

stopping power, and they're easier to set up and adjust.

If you're buying a used tandem you might want to consider this important upgrade to newer brakes. One popular upgrade is to install self-energizing brakes in the rear. They are very powerful, and counteract the effects of a tandem's long rear brake cable.

Hydraulic brakes are another alternative, and several models are now available which can be fitted to standard cantilever bosses. Instead of wire cables, hydraulic brake systems use hoses filled with fluid to activate the brakes. The result is increased stopping power and exceptionally smooth operation, especially on the long run to the rear brake.

About half of the tandems you see will have a hub brake—either a drum or disc. A non-rim brake has several advantages. It can prevent heat build-up at the rim on long descents (particularly with loaded tourists, heavier teams, or cautious captains who ride the brakes). It also gives you safety, having a third brake as a backup. And a drum's wet-weather performance doesn't diminish like that of a rim brake.

Watch out for hubs that have internal brakes. These are generally designed for single bikes and will not withstand the rigors of tandem use.

Refer to Chapter 13 for further discussion of hub brakes.

Saddles

It is very important that the stoker has a comfortable saddle. The captain is suspended in the middle of a 68-inch wheelbase and enjoys a smooth ride. The stoker sits over the rear wheel and can't anticipate the inevitable bumps and potholes. S/he needs extra protection, especially on longer rides. Make sure you get a good saddle that provides both support and shock absorption. Gel saddles or shock-absorbing saddles are used by many stokers who don't use such devices on their single bikes. It's worth repeating: unless the stoker is comfortable, a tandem will likely sit in the garage unused.

See Chapter 6 for more on stoker comfort.

Pedals

You hard-charging riders who like to pedal through sharp corners take note: catching a pedal is no fun, no matter what Al Scholz says in the upcoming racing chapter. To minimize the risk of catching a pedal (and to avoid damage to pedal spindles and crank arms), select narrow pedals.

Clipless pedals are a popular upgrade (especially for the captain) because they allow convenient entry and exit. Models which have recessed cleats prevent you from skating around on the pavement when you're holding the tandem up.

Hubs

Tandems usually come with 140mm spacing between the locknuts of the rear hub (versus 126–130mm for road bikes and 130–135mm for mountain bikes). This width is necessary if you want room for a hub brake on the left side. It has the advantage of allowing the rear wheel to be dishless (with equal spoke tension on both sides). This setup is stronger, easier to keep true, and less likely to fail than the dished wheels common on single bikes. But tandems do bend axles occasionally—not because of the wider spacing, but because of the heavier weight carried by the tandem and the larger forces transmitted through the drivetrain.

Components Equal to the Job

Tandem components live a hard life. For example, most tandem owners will tell you that the rear crank spindle is a weak point because it carries the stresses of two riders pedaling. For best results, watch for large, sealed bearings, spaced further apart than those on a single. You'll also find some tandem builders using extra-sturdy, removable seat-post binder collars on the frame. These will outlast brazed-on binders—a reassuring thought when you realize that you're saving the prospect of frame repair.

Ten years ago, tandemists had to search for good, reliable components. You now have your choice, thanks to the flurry of mountain bike developments. Brakes, headsets, derailleurs, freewheels, rims, and tires have come a long way in the past few years. They're affordable and readily available, and that's been a boon for tandems.

★ ★ ★

"He hasn't said one word about what a tandem weighs," you may think.

That's right. Single bikes are sold by the pound—or by the shedding of pounds. Tandems are not, nor should they be. On good tandems every piece of the frame and every component is made as light as possible, consistent with the durability and versatility you'll want from your tandem. When you add all those weights up, you get 35 to 45 pounds. Sure, you'll find some tandems that supposedly weigh less. If so, ask yourself two questions: One, do they really weigh less? (Who weighed it? With what kind of scale?) Two, what important features or durability did they leave off, and when would you most wish you had it? In my experience, the fastest and most enjoyable tandems weigh about 40 pounds.

★ ★ ★

Now, you're thinking that all this is going to cost you a bit of money. Good quality tandems cost over $1,000, and can easily run upwards of $2,500. Custom workmanship, aluminum frames, and other goodies can put you on the far side of $3,000. Tandems cost more to make and ship than singles because they're bulkier, the economies of manufacturing are different (i.e., worse), and there are more parts and tubing involved.

Why not buy a cheaper tandem? I think you'd be deeply disappointed with its performance. Tandems costing $500-750 come and go from the marketplace, and every one I've seen is a big disappointment. Generally, they have flexible frames, few or no frame size choices, and marginal components.

Should you buy a used tandem? Maybe, but watch out. Lots of used tandems, particularly those built before 1980, have major design flaws— far worse than you'd find in single bikes. Many are intensely uncomfortable for the stoker, with short rear top tubes and/or very slack rear seat tube angles. Some older frames and forks are so flexible that riders feel insecure on the bike.

Brakes may be marginal. Many other components from that era don't hold up.

Suppose you find a good used tandem? There are good values out there. However, the price of new tandems has dropped recently. Good used tandems hold their value so well that a good new tandem may be a better bike for the same price. Schedule a test ride of at least a half hour on the used tandem and make sure its performance and ride meet your expectations (and exceeds the performance and ride of a comparably priced new tandem).

Finally, because tandems are unusual, you need to buy yours from a shop that knows and cares about them. Ask around. Find a shop whose owner or workers ride tandems and know tandems. Arrange for a test ride of at least a half hour, away from heavy traffic. If the test ride is your first tandem experience, be sure to read the three following chapters beforehand.

4 • Riding Together Like a Pair of Pros

Watching a good tandem team is like watching champion ballroom dancers. They flow together, work together, and mesh their energies perfectly. They use the advantages of a tandem deftly to ride smoother, faster, and with more enjoyment than they ever could on single bikes.

Well, how do you get to be like that? Easy. A little practice and the right approach will make your team as smooth as any.

A team needs a good captain and a good stoker, and cooperation between them. We'll hone the captain's and stoker's skills in the next two chapters of this book. In this one, we'll look at coordination.

First of all, agree on some goals. Are you trying to ride fast and set a record, or go slow and smell the flowers? Or something in between? The captain sets the tone of the ride by bending over and sprinting at some times and sitting up and coasting at other times. S/he shifts the gears, making the decision of how high a gear to use for a given situation. Because the stoker is a captive audience, the captain's decisions along these lines should be sensitive to the stoker's desires.

A tandem can keep unequal riders together physically, but only the riders can keep themselves together mentally. This need not be difficult: I've ridden with dozens of tandem partners, some much stronger than myself, some much less strong. And I've spent plenty of time in both the front and back seats. Almost always, we learn to accommodate.

There have been times, though.... I remember one memorable century I rode with a stoker much stronger, better rested, and less hung over than myself. He just never thought I was riding hard enough. A century is a long time to put up with that kind of disagreement. We never rode together again.

Once you two have shared goals, a good captain, and a cooperative stoker, most things fall into place. Riding together smoothly seems natural. The flats whistle by underneath you, the descents whistle by faster, and the curves are exciting, as the tandem sails through smooth, steady arcs. Shifts in gearing or changes from spinning to coasting all become instinctive motions that you share with your riding partner.

Climbing hills, however, can be a grind for a not-so-harmonious tandem team. A tandem will bog down if either rider slacks off, or if coordination between the two riders is poor. So it takes a bit more mental concentration to keep your speed up on the climbs. As you approach a climb, keep pedaling smoothly and evenly. Letting up for even one pedal stroke can slow the bike down dramatically, so stay with it. Stokers should anticipate shifts and captains should announce them, so they go smoothly and quickly, and take the minimum time away from pedaling.

The good news about climbing on a tandem is that you can climb very briskly if you work together. The two of you have a lot of momentum, and that momentum can help you keep your speed up. Just don't let the momentum decay.

I've ridden many a long climb at about 20 m.p.h. My partner and I would preserve our momentum from the flats and downhills preced-ing the climb and carry that momentum all the way to the top. I've also bogged down when a partner didn't even try to save our momentum, and we've found ourselves riding our lowest gear up hills that weren't even steep.

Going fast wasn't much more work than going slow. But it demanded timing and concen-tration. So ... how fast you climb depends on how coordinated you and your partner are.

Does tandeming involve a lot of riding-related talk between captain and stoker? That's up to you. Some teams have a whole glossary of signals for each other, to signal various braking, shifting, and steering situations. I don't. The only signal I use very often is "shift," which sometimes comes out, "Lighten up, buddy!" I find that most of the other things get communi-cated nonverbally. My stoker knows what I'm trying to do—we find there's no need to say anything about it.

Both riders on a tandem tend to stay glued to their saddles more than they would on single bikes, and you need to remind yourselves to stand on the pedals, stretch your arms and legs,

Smooth spin Lulu! I think we're getting this teamwork thing down!

shrug your shoulders, and take the weight off your bum. Take turns spending ten seconds doing this every five or ten minutes. You'll be a happier team at the end of the ride.

In addition to pure fun, tandems provide a great, unique opportunity for training. Imagine being Greg LeMond's stoker for a few weeks. You'd be learning pedaling style, fitness training, and strategy all at once. And, you'd feel it through the pedals. No textbooks here: you'd be borrowing or sharing his legs and mind. If your tandem team has one experienced cyclist and one less-experienced, you have the same potential for this training.

Some people assume that it takes years of coordination for a tandem team to start and stop smoothly. But I routinely take new stokers for a ride, and we ride off as smoothly as if we'd been practicing all our lives.

So why can I start and stop smoothly, when other riders find the tandem behaving like an unruly horse? Simple: I use a simple procedure that works, and arrange things so the stoker

During startup the captain should lock the brakes and hold the bike securely while positioning her feet far enough apart to allow the stoker to move the cranks freely.

doesn't have to worry about coordinating his or her timing with mine.

To start, I shift the bike into a suitably easy gear. I then straddle the top tube (swinging my leg forward, over the handlebars, rather than back where my foot would hit bystanders in the face). Next, I grab the handlebars, lock both brakes, and plant my feet firmly on the ground, straddling the top tube. My legs are spread wide, so the pedals can rotate in between them. The bike is now securely held in an upright position. (Some captains like to actually sit on the top tube for added stability.)

Now I invite the stoker to climb on. The easiest way is for the stoker to stand to one side of the bike and position a foot in the near pedal. S/he can then use that pedal as a step and swing the other leg over the seat, as if mounting the back of a motorcycle. With both feet in the toe clips, the stoker can backpedal the cranks as necessary to get situated.

When the stoker is ready, s/he rotates the cranks so my left pedal is at the top of the power stroke (use the right if you prefer). I put one foot in that pedal's toe clip. This procedure is the same for clipless pedals, by the way.

Now it's time to shove off. I stand on the raised pedal, which starts the bike rolling. I put my other foot on the backside of the other pedal; at this time, I deliberately make no attempt to get that foot in the toe clip. I plant my bum on the saddle. After several turns of the pedals, when we're up to jogging speed, I stop pedaling and flip the other pedal around.

Note the things I don't do:

- I don't distract myself with the other toe clip until we're under way. I ignore the noise it makes scraping on the ground.
- I don't flinch at the slow speed of the first pedal stroke. I keep pointed straight ahead and keep my steering and balance corrections small.
- I don't overcorrect. (There's a big temptation to overcorrect at this point. Don't do it. Remember that overcorrection just throws your stoker's weight from side to side, and stokers don't like that.)
- I don't shift, brake, talk, or otherwise distract myself or the stoker.

When it's time to stop the bike, the same steps all take place in reverse order. When the bike stops, I slide off the saddle, take a foot out of the pedal, and put that foot on the ground.

If it's a brief stop—say, for a traffic light—I stay in that position. The stoker keeps both feet strapped in. While we're waiting, we reposition the pedals for a quick getaway. That way, there's no delay when we want to shove off again.

If we're going to dismount, I take my other foot out of the pedal and stand with both feet flat on the ground, legs spread wide to clear the pedals, brakes firmly engaged. I tell the stoker it's okay to dismount—and the stoker is free to spin the pedals while s/he dismounts. When the stoker is off the bike, s/he tells me, and I swing a leg forward over the handlebars to dismount myself.

This system works like a charm if you follow it exactly.

Occasionally you'll see a tandem with a bungee cord on each side, joining the front and rear pedals. One reason for this is to allow the tandem to be ridden alone without grinding the rear toe clips on the asphalt. It also makes it very easy for both captain and stoker to get into the pedals. Try it to see if it helps.

5 • Top Technique

Captains, you have a big responsibility with big potential rewards. Your stoker is a captive audience, completely in your hands. Want that stoker to love tandeming, and make you blush with pride by telling everyone what a great captain you are? Good. (I told you the reward was a big one.)

The steps to that reward are simple enough:

- Break your stoker in gently. Let him or her get used to what it feels like to ride on the back of a tandem. Demonstrate turning, braking, and descending so the stoker knows what those maneuvers feel like. (I described the demonstration I use in the first chapter of this book.)
- Be smooth, predictable, and precise in your maneuvers.
- Set a tone for the ride that your stoker will appreciate. If your stoker is a flower-picking tourist, ease off. If s/he is a budding young racer full of excess energy, rise to the occasion.

A stoker can't enjoy riding the way s/he likes it unless the captain cooperates!

- Be a little cautious. Bring your stoker back home without excess excitement, ride after ride. (What is "excess excitement?" It's the difference between hearing your stoker tell friends, "Wow, we went fast!" or hearing, "Wow, we almost crashed!")

Put it this way: Your biggest obligation is to make the ride pleasant for the stoker. In the long run, you'll both enjoy riding more if you make that your first priority. It avoids tension between the tandem team members.

☆ ☆ ☆

You get to make a good first impression on your stoker by getting the bike under way smoothly. Use the startup sequence described in the last chapter, and don't overcorrect your steering and balance movements during those first few slow pedal strokes.

Don't lean the bike over far to one side when you put your foot on the pedal in preparation for takeoff. Hold the bike upright, so the stoker doesn't think you're throwing him or her overboard.

Be aware that everything feels a bit different on the back seat of a tandem, and give your stoker a chance to get used to it. Demonstrate the way the bike feels at a moderate speed—10 to 15 m.p.h. That's fast enough to avoid slow-speed wobbles, but slow enough to be unexciting. At that speed, you can demonstrate turning, banking into curves, and braking. (You'll notice that you actually turn the handlebars more than you do on a single bike. It doesn't take much to get used to, though.)

A captain can make things bog down if s/he doesn't anticipate the need to shift. Maintain a good, mutually agreed-upon cadence, and watch for subtle hills or other reasons to shift to maintain that cadence. Anticipating the need to shift is more important than on a single bike, because it's much more difficult to muscle a tandem over a hill in a too-high gear. Because your stoker is a captive audience, you don't want to annoy him or her by being asleep at the shift lever.

Make a special effort to carve a nice straight path. Don't wobble or make last-minute changes in your path. If there's a pothole to dodge, start dodging early on, so your movements are gradual. (This means that you keep your eyes peeled, so you see stuff like that as far ahead as possible.)

If there's a bump, announce "Bump!" so your stoker can get some weight up out of the saddle. It's harder for the stoker to do this while pedaling than it is on a single bike, because s/he needs to pedal smoothly—so if you can stop pedaling briefly at the moment of impact, do so.

Claim a bit more of the road than you might if you were riding alone. If you skim near the right curb, next to parked cars, pavement drop-offs, or other roadside undesirables, your stoker will feel hemmed in and claustrophobic.

These guidelines are the same ones you follow when you're leading a paceline of riders on single bikes. Racers, ex-racers, and people who train in the disciplined racer format all appreciate the importance of making things predictable for following riders. A stoker on a tandem appreciates the same consideration.

The problem was my old stoker kept nagging me to pay attention....

★ ★ ★

If you want to use cleated shoes or a clipless pedal system, make sure your stoker feels comfortable with the idea first. If the stoker is worried that the captain won't be able to get out of the pedals easily, you'll generate dreaded stoker nervousness.

As you gain a little confidence, practice slow-speed maneuvering. It impresses stokers and comes in very handy. I like to do U-turns on narrow, traffic-free, two-lane roads—a useful maneuver that sure beats dismounting when we need to change direction. Go slowly, don't be surprised at how far you have to turn the bars, stay calm and still, and you'll do it like a pro.

Make sure your braking technique is good, so you can stop in the shortest distance possible without danger of skidding. The best way to learn about tandem braking technique is to compare it with single bike technique, so you know how they differ.

As I stated in the first chapter of this book, a tandem can stop shorter than a single bike. On both bikes, you get most of your braking ability from the front brake. On the single bike, the braking is limited by the possibility of pitching over the front wheel. On the tandem, your stoker's weight makes that nearly impossible.

Thus, on the tandem, the limitation is front wheel traction—just like on a car. This means your superior braking vanishes on sandy or wet surfaces. Anticipate and adjust your speed accordingly. (One possible exception: a mountain bike tandem with nice knobby tires will have good grip on the perfect dirt surface. But how do you know when the surface is perfect?)

Even so, on dry pavement, you have awesome braking power. Squeeze both brakes together, putting two or three times as much force on the front brake as on the rear brake. Never simply grab a brake lever, lest you grab too hard and initiate a skid. Instead, carefully but firmly squeeze the lever, and continuously monitor the results you get. Be sensitive to the feedback from the bike, and be ready to let up on the hand lever instantly, in the unlikely event that you squeeze too hard.

A rear wheel skid, of course, is no big deal. Just let up on the brake and hope no one noticed you shredding a perfectly good tire. A front wheel skid is considerably more sporting, since you lose the front wheel traction you need to balance the bike. Frankly, I've never skidded the front wheel on my tandem, so I can't tell you what that feels like. With due care, you'll never know what it feels like either.

You may hear people say that captaining a tandem takes a lot of upper body strength. This is a myth, and it lives on for two reasons: One, riders new to captaining a tandem tend to have sore and tired arms and shoulders after riding. Two, it's offered as an explanation why few women become tandem captains.

What you'll find, though, is that you won't get that soreness once you're used to the bike, feel less tense on it, and relax some with the job. A tandem is like any other bike—very little muscle strength is required to turn the handlebars. In certain cases, however, like riding off road or standing while climbing, you'll have to work harder to control a tandem than a single.

As for women *not* becoming captains, I have two stereotypes that might help explain: One, *some* women aren't used to forcefully taking command of a big machine whether it's a tandem or a radial arm saw. Two, *some* husbands and boyfriends who think they can do a better job make obnoxious and uphelpful stokers, despite their best intentions. (Yes, I too have been guilty at times of human weakness.)

Assuming you don't fall prey to stereotypes and myths, you'll choose your captain based not on strength but on these factors, in order of importance:

• Experience. If there's a big difference between the two riders, choose the person with the most cycling skills and tandem experience for your captain.

• Leadership. If your cycling experience is comparable, put the person with more leadership and decisiveness up front.

• Height. If your experience and leadership levels are near equal, don't fight it out. Choose the taller cyclist as captain. Most tandems have a rearward sloping top tube, which anticipates a smaller stoker.

• Weight. Last but still important, tandems generally handle better if the captain is the larger and heavier of the two.

I do rank experience far above size and weight in importance. I sometimes captain stokers up to 50 pounds and/or 8 inches bigger than myself, and we make a fine team. (They are thoroughly warned about not throwing their weight around.) By the same token, out of politeness, I've sat in back for a couple of big, but absolutely clueless novice riders who thought they should be captain because of size alone. All I could think of was, "Boy, if we switched seats for ten minutes, you'd learn so much."

If you and your tandem partner have comparable skills, you have an embarrassment of riches: you can switch off! ("It's your turn to do all the work; I wanna play with the binoculars.") Try both ways. You'll both learn why you don't want the other person to be a back-seat driver.

6 • Stoker Tips

Once you've established your agreed-upon style of riding, the stoker has two duties: to relax and to follow the captain. No one has any fun when the stoker tries to steer the bike, second-guess the captain, or fight the flow the captain has established. Again, it's like ballroom dancing: someone has to lead, and someone has to follow.

It will only take a little practice to follow gracefully. Every bike rider stops pedaling abruptly when it's time to coast, and tandem captains are no exception. Amazingly, though, if you have a good stoker mindset, you won't find this disorienting or bothersome. When the captain pours on the coals, so do you. As soon as the captain stops pedaling, your legs go limp. (And they should go limp; the captain may need to lift the inside pedal to bank steeply around the corner, and s/he should never have to fight the stoker to do so.)

The captain may need to brake sharply, without time to tell you about it. ("Hey, get this! A cow is crossing the road 20 feet in front of us....") The stoker must be ready to hang on when that happens.

Similarly, the captain can't make a committee decision with the stoker about exactly where s/he steers the bike. The stoker should follow and lean with the flow (but not overdo it). If you're riding with a good captain, s/he deserves this confidence.

Both stoker and captain will enjoy a smoother ride if both avoid unnecessary body motion. As your legs churn and deliver the power, your upper bodies should be relaxed and almost motionless.

The previous chapter tells captains how to pamper stokers and gain their confidence. Read it to see what the captain is up to. But if you're a wee bit nervous about being a stoker, how do you get over it? Easy. Here are a few thoughts that will reassure you.

First, riding a tandem is the only time you will be riding a bike when you have minimal responsibility for balancing it. Any bike moves slightly from side to side as the rider nudges the handlebars to make balance corrections. New stokers may find this disconcerting, because they aren't used to these movements being performed for them. Relax. Once you realize that this is just part of riding a tandem, you'll get accustomed to it.

After you get used to the sensation of someone else balancing the bike, everything else makes more sense. Sure, that person is in control and you're not—but the same is true when you're a passenger in any other vehicle. And you'll soon develop a feel for the rhythm of the captain's movements. You can enhance or break that rhythm. If the captain sighs before downshifts, you'll know when to expect a downshift. If s/he leans forward before braking, you'll know when to expect a stop. And so on.

Although it's great fun to be a stoker, there's one catch: the ride in the back seat usually *feels* bumpier than the front. There are two main reasons for this: First, tandem frames generally have heavy-duty stays and more bracing at the rear seat tube, which translates into a less forgiving ride. Second, the stoker can't see what's

coming, so the bumps feel more pronounced. You know what it's like to walk down a flight of stairs, and find one more step than you expected? The last step can be quite jarring, simply because you aren't prepared for it.

Fortunately, some simple modifications can make the rear quarters of your tandem just as cozy as your favorite single bike. Fitting wider tires is a good first step. Most tandems have room for wider tires than the ones that come stock. Tandems weigh more than single bikes and carry heavier loads, so it's logical to use tires with a wider profile and a bigger air volume. Of course, a fatter tire not only smooths out the bumps in the road, it also reduces your risk of pinch flats. The downside is that wide tires have slightly more rolling resistance than skinny tires, but this effect is minimal relative to the extra horsepower of a tandem.

Some stokers further increase their comfort margin with a well-padded saddle or gel saddle pad. A more sophisticated approach to comfort, especially on longer rides or bumpy roads, is to employ a shock-absorbing seatpost. There are a wide range of brands now available, including Hydrapost and Roll-r-Post. These suspension mechanisms range from simple elastomers (rubber bumpers) to air-sprung, oil-damped suspension units. A successful variation is the Allsop Softride system, which eliminates the seatpost entirely in favor of a carbon-fiber cantilever beam.

In an ideal world, the stoker would always keep both hands on the handlebars at all times. And that's for good reason: You don't want to get jolted from your saddle if your captain has to make a quick emergency maneuver. But in the real world, there is water to drink, hand signals to make, and pictures to take. No matter what I tell you, you'll take a hand off for these and other purposes. So I will tell you

this: There's always a small risk in taking a hand off the bars. Even on the quietest road, a jackrabbit or unnoticed pothole can intrude. So when you do take your hands off the bars, be smart about it. Let your captain know, and keep at least one hand on the bars if you have any choice. Wait for a quiet stretch of road, where

The Allsop beam pictured here, or a variety of shock-absorbing seatposts, can help provide greater stoker comfort.

intrusions are less likely, and remain prepared for those intrusions. Be mentally ready to drop whatever it is you're fiddling with (yes, even the camera) and grab the bars.

Fear of the unknown is all you need to overcome to be a happy stoker. You'll find it an easy transition.

Hone your skills at mentally anticipating and physically following through with the captain's movements. You'll play a big part in making the ride smoother for both of you.

Here are some additional do's and don'ts for stokers:

• Do double-tie your shoelaces. Better yet, stuff your laces into your shoes.

• Don't climb onto the bike until you've finished knotting and tucking your shoelaces. You have shoelace-eating chains and chainrings on both sides, and the left chainring is especially hungry. Because the left chainring is open at the front it tends to grab and eat shoelaces much more than you're used to. It's no fun to get wrapped up as you're pedaling along—and, of course, it could be dangerous.

• Don't scratch your back, wiggle, or make abrupt and unexpected moves. It could cause the bike to veer a foot or two to the side. Depending on what's a foot or two next to you, abrupt moves can be dangerous.

• Don't wiggle while sitting clipped in at stop signs; you risk throwing the captain off balance and falling over.

If, after this description, you feel like the stoker still needs more duties, I can think of several. Earlier I mentioned taking pictures. The stoker can also be in charge of the snacks, daily weather report, newspaper, transistor radio, and other goodies stored in the captain's jersey pocket or stoker's handlebar bag. When a navigation question arises, spread a map out all over the captain's back!

7 • Bringing the Family

There's a cute little lakeside park a few miles out of town. What better way to spend your time than taking the family for a bike ride out there for a picnic?

And what better way to take a bike ride than to go on your tandem, with your children securely strapped into a bike trailer?

It can be a lot of fun.

Of course, if it's mishandled it can also be an opportunity for a family-wide misunderstanding. Here are some tips to keep your family happy fellow-travelers.

For children from 18 months through five or so, the way to travel is in a trailer. Older children up to age ten will want to ride on the back of the tandem with a childback conversion.

Young babies less than 18 months may not be ready for trailer riding because they may not have the strength to hold their heads up for the duration of the ride. (And the helmet, which you wouldn't leave home without, does add a little

A trailer provides the perfect means for making a day of cycling a whole family affair.

weight to the child's head.) Do check carefully before taking a youngster on a bike ride, and ask the child's doctor if you have any doubt.

Riding with parents is a very special treat for children. They get to see the scenery at a moderate open-air pace and enjoy a fresh-air outing with their parents. My own children love riding in their trailer. When my daughter was first learning to talk, some of the first words she learned to say were how to ask for a trailer ride. On sunny afternoons, she'd eagerly grab her helmet and say, "Marie's helmet—Daddy, go bike!"

I love to look at the trailers owned by avid family cycling enthusiasts. The insides of the trailer are loaded with stuffed animals, children's books, snacks, water bottle cages, and fruit juice. Some are very elaborate little play environments.

When your children are in the trailer, you can enjoy tandeming much as you would before you had children. Sure, you go slower up hills because the trailer slows you down, and you go slower down hills because you're a safe and prudent kind of person. But you still enjoy the fun of togetherness, and you can go on rides of substantial duration while your children entertain themselves in the caboose.

The trailer is the safest way to bring kids along by bicycle. The alternative, a bike-mounted child seat, has three drawbacks:

One, it places the child's weight high, and behind the rear axle. This hurts the handling and stability of the bike, particularly on a single bike. Two, if you have a mishap and the bike falls over, the child seat falls from a height of about three feet. And three, there's very little rollover protection for the child inside.

A good trailer neatly solves these problems. The rear axle mount affects the handling of your bike so little that you'll find yourself looking behind you to make sure the trailer is still attached. Also, the trailer is low, with the child less than a foot above the ground, and its low center of gravity usually keeps it upright even if the bicycle manages to fall over. If the bicycle does pull the trailer over, the child doesn't fall from any distance—rather, the worst that can

A childback conversion clamps onto the stoker's seat tube and uses a downsized crankset, allowing kids to reach the pedals.

happen is that the trailer turns over sideways, usually in slow motion. And the trailer has a good roll cage.

Some people may be concerned that the trailer is difficult for other road users to see, or that it's too wide. Neither of these is a problem. Good trailers are made in bright colors, with a flag as standard equipment. People will notice you! And at less than a yard wide you'll find that road sharing normally isn't a problem. If motorists give you funny looks, it will be because they're curious, and perhaps envious of the fun you're having.

When will the child be too old for the trailer? You'll probably make that decision yourself—you'll want the kid (who gets heavier every year) to get out and help pedal!

Around five or so, a child is typically ready for a childback conversion on a tandem—and this can be a spectacular treat for the child. Now the child isn't just being brought along—s/he is participating! The kids will love it.

Do remember, though, that once your child moves onto the bike, you have to accommodate the child's exercise goals—which are probably minimal. Kids like to get out and have a good time, but they also like to stop and explore things. They aren't the least bit interested in plodding along to develop their aerobic fitness, and telling them about it won't change their minds.

Be careful not to push your child's endurance. Young children in particular can lose interest and might even nod off on too long a ride.

Enjoy your child's spontaneity. Don't think that you have to ride to X because that's what you set out to do. Feel free to stop and climb a tree, catch frogs, or sit around a picnic table. That's how you get your children to enjoy cycling.

If you're the kind of rider who likes to hammer on a bike for long stretches, your first reaction may be that it is frustrating to take your kids along. There's an easy and effective answer to that: Don't think of family cycling as exercise for yourself. Think of it as a family fun activity, like going to the zoo. Any exercise you get for yourself is a bonus.

It's best if the ride has a purpose for the children. It can be as simple as visiting a friend across town, or buying a few groceries. You can go see the new ponies at the local farm, go to the fair, or bring that picnic along.

Start out with short rides of just a few miles, to get yourself and your children accustomed to the new traveling arrangements. You'll soon find yourself wanting to go on longer and longer outings. Just remember not to schedule rides so long they exhaust your children's patience.

One of the benefits of riding with your children is that you'll be teaching them good technique and safe riding habits. Most parents never ride with their children. By providing a role model, you'll help them learn to ride safely later on when you're not there.

Get helmets for the whole family. To me, taking a child cycling without a helmet is comparable to tossing him or her in the back seat of your car and saying "hold on" as you speed off. It's something you just don't do.

The best way to see the fun and excitement of family cycling is to attend one of the many

From an early age, kids can learn about cycling firsthand and even pull their own weight using a childback conversion.

regional weekend tandem rallies held each summer in the U.S. My family often attends the Eastern Tandem Rally and Family Cycling Association weekends.

Tandem rallies attract all kinds of riders: older couples, strapping young athletes, and families with kids. Lots of kids. You'll see trailers, childback conversions, children on single bikes, and even triples. And you'll see many great examples of families enjoying the time they spend cycling together. The tandem rallies I'm familiar with are non-competitive events, with different ride distances available for everyone from the very strongest to the most deskbound riders. And the Eastern Tandem Rally has a tradition of gourmet food.

To learn about tandem rallies and other events, join the Tandem Club of America (TCA) and read their publications. TCA publishes a list of tandem rallies sponsored by a number of tandem clubs and organizations around the country. See the Appendix for TCA's address.

(Thanks to Harvey Sachs, my family cycling mentor, for help with this chapter.)

8 • Tandem Touring

Tandem touring is an elegant way to travel. People you encounter will smile and wave, roll down their car windows and sing, "Bicycle Built for Two," and want to know more about you. You can expect a cordial greeting from innkeepers when you roll up to their front porch, or an envious eye from tourists on single bikes at campgrounds.

Sure, bicycle touring has always been a good conversation starter for travelers, but riding a tandem gets you past the "How many flats?" kind of conversation. People are more interested in you and your riding partner. The conversations you'll have will make it easier for you to learn about the people and places you're visiting.

Tandem touring is also where you really appreciate the advantage of staying together without having to struggle to coordinate your riding. Sure, it's an advantage for a short ride around home, but that advantage is magnified when you're riding all day long.

The nuts-and-bolts aspects of tandem touring are quite simple. If anything, they are easier than they are for touring on single bikes. Front and rear panniers give you plenty of room for your gear; rear panniers alone are probably sufficient for short inn-to-inn tours.

The surprisingly good news is that weight distribution of touring loads on a tandem is less critical than on a single bike. The main problem on single bikes is that rear panniers put almost all their weight behind the rear axle. This can cause a single bike to handle poorly.

But on a tandem, weight in your rear panniers doesn't affect handling very much because you have a much longer wheelbase, with so much weight between the axles. Frankly, I can hardly tell the difference in handling.

(Of course, a huge, overloaded handlebar bag can hurt a tandem's steering. But you won't need a huge handlebar bag with all that other space. You can keep maps, sunglasses, small camera and binoculars, and other lightweight items in a tiny handlebar bag.)

If you need to bring more gear, items like spare tires can be tied to the space within the frame. We've even known tandem touring enthusiasts who have made their own in-frame bags to carry tools and other heavy items.

In several instances a trailer can be your ultimate solution. If you bring your child, plan on using a good, lightweight trailer. Also, a trailer is a great option if you're going on a longer tour, just don't like traveling light, or want to preserve your unloaded bike's handling characteristics.

Whether you opt for a trailer or for panniers, you'll find your bike is easy to ride. Sure, it climbs slowly, but that just means you have plenty of time to admire the mountainside vistas and talk about them with your partner. Besides, all that weight makes it descend like an anvil dropping down a mine shaft. (This is the time that an optional hub brake comes in handy.)

A loaded tandem's main pitfall is this: If you lean the bike over to one side when mounting or dismounting, the extra weight may become difficult to control. When parking a loaded tandem, a hub brake operated by a shift lever has the added advantage of acting as a parking brake. See Chapter 13 for more on this.

A tandem that's loaded with touring gear handles much like an unloaded tandem. One reason the load makes less difference on a tandem than on a single has to do with the ratio of sprung to unsprung weight. Sprung weight refers to the parts of a vehicle and its contents which are isolated from the road by suspension. On a typical bicycle, the entire bike is unsprung weight, whereas the rider's weight is sprung because the arms and legs act like shock absorbers.

An unloaded single bike has very little unsprung weight—simply the weight of the bike itself. But when the bike is loaded with bags, it has significantly more unsprung weight (perhaps twice as much) which tends to alter the handling drastically.

But everything works out differently on a tandem. The bike itself is heavier, and the captain and stoker spend more time seated. The overall result is much more unsprung weight. So loading the tandem with bags doesn't have much effect.

The fact that your body weight is unsprung on a tandem leads to the only essential admonition for tandem touring: Get off the bike more frequently than you might on single bikes. (For some people, that means every 20 minutes; for others, that means every six hours. Decide where you and your partner fit in.) Massage each other's shoulders and back. Massage and ventilate your um ... er ... area of saddle contact so it doesn't get sore from too much pressure for too long. And don't rib your stoker if s/he wants a gel padded seat cushion or a shock-absorbing seatpost on long rides.

Do these things and you'll find tandem touring an incredibly beautiful way to see the countryside.

Traveling with Your Tandem

It's easier than you think! Here are a few hints: Minivans and pickup trucks make quite usable tandem transports. (One caveat—don't just lay your tandem in the bed of a pickup truck. It must be tied down. I learned this the hard way. When the truck went over a bump, my beloved tandem flew up and landed with such force that it bent a very expensive crank arm.)

Roof racks are now so widely available and convenient to use that we need only say, "Go see your authorized dealer." Several top brands cater to tandemists.

Putting a tandem on a roof rack can be harrowing if you do it wrong. Doing it right doesn't require much strength, provided you have a helper and use a systematic approach. I always do mine exactly the same way, following the same steps in the same order.

Putting a tandem on the roof is a two-person job. Because I do it systematically, I can easily have a stranger help me if my stoker is otherwise occupied. The process goes like this: Lock the rear wheel. If you have a hub brake actuated by a thumb shifter, you can use it to lock the wheel. Otherwise, squeeze the brake lever and jam a coin or small block of wood in the brake lever to keep the wheel locked. Station yourself at the front of the tandem, with the helper at the rear. Have your helper grasp the tandem by the rear wheel. (When the bike is high up on the roof, that's the only place that's easy for your helper to reach.) You grasp the tandem by the head tube area in one hand, and front forks or handlebars in the other hand. The two of you pick the tandem up and lift it over the rack. You should have the car door open so you can step up on the doorsill to help extend your reach as you lift the front of the bike while your helper stays behind the car.

For racks that use a removed front wheel, have your helper hold the rear of the bike up high while you insert the front forks into the rack's fork-locking mechanism. Have your friend gently lower the rear of the bike so it is sitting on its part of the rack. Tighten the front quick release, then tighten the rear tiedown mechanism.

For racks that hold the tandem with the front wheel in place, locate both wheels in the track. Have your helper hold the bike upright while you attach the bike to one of the upright mechanisms, then tighten the other mechanism.

To remove the tandem from the rack, simply reverse this process.

Airlines

Ah, those rapacious airlines, with their extra fees for taking a bicycle. Here's how to work them to your advantage:

Always arrive early, with your bike boxed, securely taped and sealed and ready to go. (Don't forget your name, address, and phone number, in foot-high letters on the outside.) Keep in mind that a boxed tandem is big, so transporting it to the airport takes extra time and may require a truck or minivan.

If there's a curbside check-in station, and you tip the personnel generously (like $10 or $20), there's a chance they'll "forget" to charge you the extra baggage fee. One cyclist we know gets his triple checked as regular baggage this way.

Most riders stuff their other baggage in the box with the tandem. It's possible to put all your gear in that large box, along with your tandem, so the two of you travel with only the one box and your carry-on bags. This is convenient for you and convenient for the airline. One word of

We've got two bags and a carry on!!!

caution: be sure to verify weight limits before you try to check-in.

Don't mention that you have a tandem. "Yes, it's a bicycle," is all you need say. Generally, they won't ask, and generally there aren't special exclusions for tandems. An occasional baggage handler may mumble, "Gee, that's a big box," but the boxes the airlines provide for single bikes are sometimes bigger!

Tandem boxes are difficult to come by, and finding a place to store your box can present a challenge. If you are touring and plan to cycle away from the airport, talk to the people in baggage claim and see if they can store your box. Larger airports have "left luggage" desks where you can check bags (and empty boxes) for a few dollars per day. If you run into size limits or other regulations, tell the baggage personnel your plans ("... we've got a tandem and are going to cycle though your beautiful countryside for two weeks"), and they'll likely accommodate you. You may need to collapse and fold the box so it takes up less space.

If you are going into the city before cycling, it will take some effort to find a taxi or bus that accepts your boxed tandem. Persistence and persuasion are your best tools here. Most hotels will store your box until you return. Or, if you find a bike shop with hours that match your itinerary, they're almost always ready to help store your box.

Sometimes you have to throw your box away; for instance when you arrive and depart in different cities. If you can't find a tandem box when departing, get two single boxes from a bike shop and tie and tape them together. Figure 8.1 shows a good strong joint for the overlapping boxes.

Without regard to where (or if) you keep your box, bring packing tape and rope for your return trip. Don't rely on airport gift shops or check-in counters to bail you out.

As an alternative to boxes, some very elegant carrying bags are also available. The trend in bag design is to reduce the exterior size of the bag by having you disassemble the bike fairly completely.

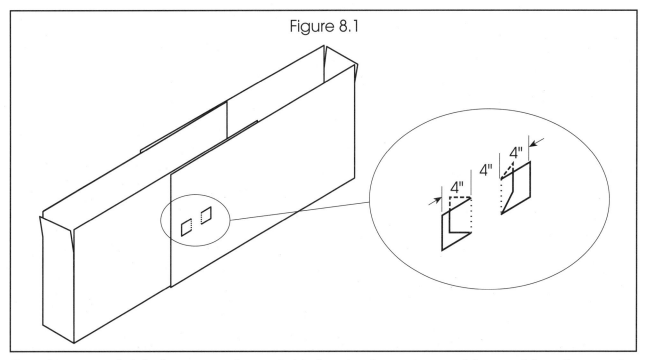

Figure 8.1

To make two single bike boxes into a box suitable for a tandem, cut one end from each box, then overlap them as shown. Next, cut through both boxes on the solid line, and fold flaps inward at dotted line so they overlap. Finally, wrap tape or tie rope around the flaps. Use this procedure on both sides.

International flights are a different, and vastly superior, kettle of fish. There is no excess baggage charge! (But make sure you check your bike all the way through or the airline may try to charge you excess baggage for the domestic portion of the flight.) Some international airlines will take your tandem unboxed, with the pedals removed and handlebars turned sideways, but don't rely on this unless it's an emergency and you're indifferent about your bike's paint job.

International flights offer a new challenge: Customs—and those five-mile hikes through international terminals. Most airports have hand-carts, so you can push, rather than carry, your boxed tandem down those endless corridors. It helps if one person navigates so you don't plow down other travelers. If you travel often, you might want to make a small cart out of old roller skates or furniture casters and a one-foot-square piece of wood.

One potential problem with any bike, single or tandem, is fitting it through security scanners. Be prepared to unbox your bike for manual inspection (remember, arrive extra early).

In most of Europe, your unboxed tandem can ride with you on the train after you remove its pedals.

Ask your travel agent for details regarding individual airlines and train lines.

One way to beat the airline baggage fees is to belong to a cycling organization which has negotiated a special deal with one or more airlines. The best such deal we know of is available to members of the League of American Wheelmen (address in the Appendix). Join the League, buy your plane tickets through their special travel agent, fly any of the four major airlines they've contracted with, and your bike flies free. Again, don't mention that it's a tandem.

The United States Cycling Federation (USCF) has a special deal for cyclists flying to/from USCF races. Bikecentennial has a travel agent who specializes in trips with bicycles, and Bikecentennial's Cyclists' Yellow Pages (free to all members) has a list of bicycle policies for all major domestic and international airlines, together with addresses and phone numbers. (Addresses for both of these organizations are in the Appendix.)

9 • Mountain Tandeming

A mountain bike tandem can take two of you on day rides or multi-day tours that no ordinary tandem can tackle. Dirt roads? No problem. Logging roads and fire trails? Instead of groaning, "We can't ride over this stuff," you'll smile inside and say, "That's where the best scenery is!"

Talk about getting away from it all.

Most of the trails which single riders enjoy on mountain bikes are accessible to a fat-tire tandem. But just so we don't overstate the case, the most challenging mountain bike trails are generally too technically difficult for tandemists. You can't ride a tandem over trails which require the rider to get up and hop the wheel(s) over rocks and roots. The weight-shifting and wheel-lifting exercises which are part of technical mountain bike riding are not possible on a tandem. And because a tandem has a larger turning circle, it can't handle the sharpest switchback turns on single-track trails.

Off-road tandeming provides its own rewards—and requires its own unique riding strategies.

Even so, mountain tandems have some real advantages over singles which help even the score on trails of average difficulty. On extemely steep climbs, riders on single bikes must carefully shift their weight to keep the front wheel down without losing traction in the rear. But the extra weight on a tandem helps keep both wheels planted on terra firma, and as long as you and your partner can keep the pedals turning, you can power up all sorts of impossibly steep ascents (provided you've got some super-low gears).

Conversely, when the trail dips down, a tandem is much less likely to launch you over the bars than a single—because the stoker's weight keeps the rear of the bike from tipping up when the brakes are applied.

OK … so a mountain tandem can't go everywhere mountain singles go. I've found that when it comes to off-road riding, the limiting factor is not so much the tandem itself, but the skill (and chutzpah) of the riders.

For many, the allure of riding a tandem off-road isn't based so much on pure speed. Rather, the challenge of coordinating riding skills and negotiating trails with a long wheelbase can be as much fun as zipping along on the open road.

If you're taking a tandem off-road for the first time, try to limit your riding to trails that aren't too technical. Here's one handy rule of thumb: if novice riders get through the ride on single mountain bikes, or if riders with loaded panniers can, a tandem can too.

Bear in mind that a tandem's extra weight will require different technique. In dirt, gravel, mud, or snow your mountain tandem will want to keep going straight. So plan on taking those sharp turns at the bottom of a fast descent with caution.

Stoker backside comfort, a potential sore point on paved roads, is even more tenuous off-road. As stoker, you'll want to crouch forward, particularly when coasting or descending. Don't plant your weight on the saddle, pedals, or handlebars; instead, stay loose. As captain, avoid all bad bumps, and call out the ones you can't avoid.

Of course, many riders use mountain bikes for all kinds of riding, including riding on pavement. The mountain tandem is superb for this; it gives greater comfort than road tandems because of the shock absorption in the tires and the more upright riding position. And when the pavement ends, you just smile and look forward to better scenery.

One important thing about sizing: If you ride your mountain tandem mostly on paved surfaces, it should be sized about two inches smaller than a road bike to allow for added straddle clearance and a higher bottom bracket (straddle height being equal, a higher bottom

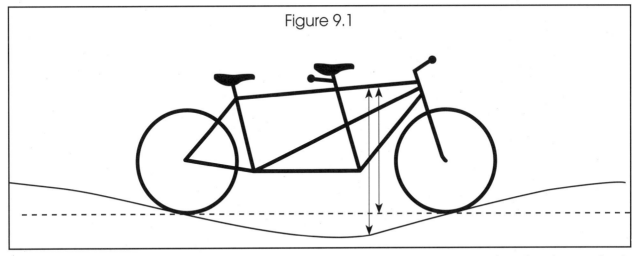

Figure 9.1

When purchasing a tandem for off-road use, be aware that uneven terrain, combined with a tandem's long wheelbase, may require additional standover for the captain.

bracket shortens the seat tube length, which is how bikes are sized). If you foresee using your mountain tandem on trails, the captain's frame size should be three or more inches smaller than a road bike—even smaller than your mountain single, if possible. That's because you can get a wider, deeper ravine under the long wheelbase of a mountain tandem, so a little extra straddle clearance can come in handy when the going gets gnarly (see Figure 9.1).

The book is still being written on how riders use mountain bike tandems. Certainly, they can fulfill missions that no other bike can, and they'll inspire riders to invent new missions. How you use yours is really up to your own imagination. Send me a card (care of the publisher) from some faraway place, and let me know how you've stretched the sport of cycling with your mountain tandem.

10 • Tandem Racing

By Alan Scholz with John Schubert

Everything that makes tandeming an improvement over single bike riding applies to racing as well. It's faster, more exciting, and there's more teamwork involved. And tandem racing, although rare, is starting to become less so (particularly on the West Coast).

Most people are familiar with three forms of tandem racing: the five-lap velodrome sprint races on special track tandems, tandem time trials, and the tandem stage race.

But even if none of these events is available to you, there are many reasons why you may want to learn tandem racing techniques.

One thing that's particularly positive about tandem racing is that it rewards teamwork. Two ordinary riders who work together well can overpower two strong riders who fight each other. We've seen that in the Duet Cycling Classic, where one heavily favored team had two national-class riders, one of them sporting a silver

A spectator's view from the criterium of the Duet Cycling Classic—an annual tandems-only stage race in Eugene, Oregon.

medal from the National Time Trial Championships. The other riders all told each other, "Well, we're racing for second place this year." But the time-trial champs weren't used to riding together and finished fourth, despite their superior horsepower.

A husband/wife team, if they ride like a true team, can compete favorably with teams composed of two strong men. My wife and I have done exactly that in two of the Duet Cycling Classics. One "mixed doubles" team won the Duet Cycling Classic criterium—in a field sprint, no less!

Another rewarding aspect of tandem racing is that it teaches racing skills and tactics quickly. This holds true even when you're among single bikes in a club training race or paceline ride. By riding stoker with an experienced captain, a new prospective racer will learn how to spin in the first two days. Within a few weeks, the stoker will have absorbed all the captain's seasoned judgment about when to attack, when to wait and rest, when to shift, how to draft for maximum energy savings, how to avoid dangerous spots in the peloton, and how to avoid crashing. The new

rider will have experienced the thrill of staying with the peloton and taking a pull at the front. On his or her single bike, that rider would have only experienced the grief of getting dropped.

Because tandem racing offers such a drastic shortcut into the sport for new riders, it's enticing for people who would never race on single bikes. My wife, for example, is a darn good criterium racer—but she'd never race on a single bike.

Tandem racing is generally friendlier than single bike racing. To begin with, every captain is responsible for his or her stoker. That responsibility discourages reckless behavior. And riders are always talking to their partners, whispering to discuss tactics. So there's less of a "me against everybody" attitude. Riders tend to be more careful, allowing more space on either side than single bike riders, and actually looking back before pulling over in front of another tandem. (This latter move is essential, given the extra length of the tandem.) Yet, when riding directly behind another tandem, riders tend to be as close as they would on singles (4 to 12 inches).

Despite the aerodynamic efficiency of tandems, racers still take advantage of their rivals' slipstream to conserve energy.

One reason why: a tandem doesn't twitch and surge as much as a single, so the wheel you're following is more predictable.

Overall, tandem racing is like riding in a civilized master's race. There have been very few crashes at the Duet Cycling Classic, which is something I can't say about most single bike races.

Tandem track racing is a special case, partly because it's so rare and partly because it's only appropriate for a few ultra-gifted sprinters. Too often the five-lap sprint race is a sideline event for single bike track sprinters who have very little tandem experience. Two riders are shoehorned onto a short, cramped tandem (made short to enhance its maneuverability), and they trust their lives to awesomely overinflated sew-up tires. Maneuvering a tandem is no piece of cake for a tandem captain on a velodrome's steep (typically 28-degree) banking, and so if a track tandem captain is inexperienced s/he'll tend to produce conservative, somewhat boring races. But the good tandem racers in this country make tandem night at the velodrome the highlight of the season. These riders delight the crowd with daring attacks, awesome jockeying for position, and bursts of speed. Only the last 200 meters of the five-lap race are timed, since most of the five laps are spent in slow-speed jockeying for favorable position. Those 200-meter times frequently calculate to well over 40 m.p.h.

In road racing, tandems still suffer from their relative rarity. The largest tandem field I've ever raced in had 26 bikes, and in a field that small, one sees both the front and the rear of the pack much more often than in a Senior Men's field with over 100 entrants. Every tandem gets to take its turn at the front. The field moves around more slowly, since maneuvers such as lane changes take longer on tandems. In corners, the field is fast but not volatile. When you start cornering a tandem, there's not much temptation to change your line. The bike itself is predictable, and it will follow the line you initially select. Compare that with a Cat. IV field, full of nervous first-time racers on expensive, twitchy single bikes!

Tandem road races have breakaways, just like single bike races. Groups of two to four tandems can work together well and smoke the field.

Like any bike, a tandem will corner at angles up to 45 degrees. But of greater interest is the maximum angle at which the tandem can be pedaled through corners—somewhere around 28 degrees, depending on the bike. The more fearless riders benefit from the way a tandem behaves when you strike the inside pedal in hard cornering: the rear wheel hops about four inches sideways, but your balance is nearly intact. You just reduce your lean angle and keep riding. The biggest damage is to your now-fearful stoker's blood pressure—who, when s/he stops shaking, will give you quite the tongue lashing. On a single, a four-inch hop makes a crash inevitable. [Editor's note: It is less likely but quite possible that a tandem will crash when it strikes a pedal going through a turn. As in any bike racing, be prepared for the consequences when you push the limit.]

Mixed tandem racing offers a unique opportunity for men and women to compete together as a team.

Any tactical maneuver on a tandem takes more planning than on a single. On a single, when you want to attack, you just do it. In a tandem pack, you hear whispers all the time ("How do you feel? Are you ready to go?").

And although it might seem cumbersome to have to consult your stoker before attacking, therein lies one of the advantages of tandeming. You can use your stoker like a set of afterburners, to kick in at key times for maximum tactical advantage. The trick is to keep the stoker underworked most of the race.

I often tell my stoker, "Take it easy, everything's fine. Rest here. Wait; we're not trying to get away yet." Keep the stoker in reserve. Don't have your stoker go all out unless you really need to; s/he'll be champing at the bit and ready to go. When a stoker feels like s/he hasn't ridden hard enough, s/he will be well warmed up, well rested, and impatient. When you ask for all s/he's got, you'll get a boost of speed that you can use to enormous tactical advantage. You can jump far ahead of the field quickly.

But on the other hand, an ill-coordinated attack is embarrassing. Two tired riders slowly wallow off the front, where the rest of the field can watch them tire themselves out.

It takes finesse to use your stoker's energy wisely. Most stokers will always push hard if you ask them to, and they won't complain of fatigue until they're completely worn out. So don't count on the stoker to employ strength strategically. That's the captain's job.

When it's time for the field sprint, several factors come into play. One is the stoker's afterburners, which you've wisely saved for this moment. Another is the extra wind resistance of a 38 m.p.h. field sprint (compared with, say, 33 m.p.h. in your average single bike race). A third is the extra length of a tandem, which makes it harder to jump past a bike you've been drafting.

What all of this means is that tandems can have 200-meter field sprints, like single bikes. Or one can start the sprint at 500 meters, tire, and get passed inside the 200-meter mark. Or a crafty tandem team can control the sprint for the full 500 meters and win the sprint.

Normally, if you sprint at 500 meters, you'll be too tired to hold your lead. But what you can do instead is this: Prearrange the sprint with your stoker. At 500 meters, you roll up to speed, making sure you've picked the best line. The other tandems will all react, but you have two advantages: you're already up to speed and in the best position. At 200 meters, you remind the stoker that it's his or her turn to burn. The stoker puts in the best pedal strokes of the day to maintain your speed. Any other tandem team that wants to pass you will have to take a less favorable line through the corner, face the wind resistance at a speed even greater than yours, and get around your nine-foot length. What you hope is that the other captain will time the sprint as if s/he were on a single bike and only had to pass a five-foot bike. If the other captain obliges you, you'll cross the line several feet in front.

Tandems have a reputation for climbing slowly, and that just ain't so. A team that works together can climb very quickly. (I have always had my cranks in phase for fast climbing.) Standing climbing is a maneuver that takes lots of

You see Chet, it takes more than great quads and VO$_2$ max uptake!

practice and lots of coordination. For the captain, it takes more upper-body strength than on a single bike, since you have to work the handlebars so hard. We find that on the tandem, we stand up much less than we would on single bikes.

In my club race series, all the records are held by tandems. The races amount to all the singles "ganging up" against the tandem; still, the tandem pulls away from the entire pack of singles, with a speed advantage of about two m.p.h.

Of course, tandems do live up to their reputation for fast descending. At the Duet Cycling Classic, tandems have been clocked at over 60 m.p.h. descending an eight percent (moderately steep) grade.

One time-honored place where tandems strut their stuff is in long rides such as the Davis Double Century, where tandems and singles start together, but tandems dominate the fastest finish times. Strong riders turn in eight-hour times for double centuries!

The competition in these events can be pretty serious, and a powerful tandem team doesn't want the rest of the field to draft the tandem to the finish line. The best way to do that is to have a teammate on a single bike sitting on your wheel and keeping anyone else from doing likewise. This teammate is called the "scrub." The scrub hogs the sweet spot drafting the tandem's wheel. Other bikes inevitably fall in line behind the scrub. To shake them off, the tandem and the scrub engage in pre-rehearsed sprinting and jumping maneuvers. The scrub allows a 20-foot gap to open, and then sprints abruptly to get back on the tandem's wheel. As soon as the scrub gets back on the tandem's wheel, the three riders hammer. The other riders are caught by surprise, and by the time they can react, the gap is too large for them to cross. Suddenly, they're out of the tandem's draft, and they can't keep up.

If you're fortunate enough to have a good stiff crosswind, another tactic is to take a position on the downwind edge of the pavement and sprint away. Because your wind shadow is beside you, no one can draft you without riding on the dirt beside the road. (Sometimes, determined riders do exactly that!) Single riders use this tactic, but it is especially suited to tandems, which have the power and aerodynamic advantage to pull off a sustained breakaway.

So what's it take to be a well-coordinated tandem racing team? It depends more on attitude than miles spent riding together. Good riders, particularly those with other tandem experience, can become a fluent team quickly. They learn to telegraph their intentions through their feet. Coasting, shifting, and other mundane maneuvers happen quickly and fluidly when riders think ahead.

Now, this isn't a license to enter a race with only once-around-the-block experience. A competitive racing team will have a minimum of several hundred miles together—and perhaps much more, depending on how they learn to ride together. Tourists and century riders won't require as much experience together to perform comfortably, but they won't be sprinting elbow-to-elbow at 40 m.p.h. either.

Equipment durability has been a factor in every race I've ever seen. You want strong stuff that won't break. I've seen broken crank spindles, snapped chains, flats, bent wheels, and failed derailleurs. Of course, there's no excuse for starting a race with old,

Sprinting out of the saddle in a tandem pack is a supreme test of team coordination and the captain's bike-handling skill.

worn-out equipment, but some equipment designs last longer than others. To cite one of my favorite examples, I prefer crank spindles with pressed-in bearings, rather than the more common screwed-in bearing cups. The pressed-in style supports the crank spindle nearer the load, reducing the strain on the spindle.

I also prefer 26-inch rims. Because their diameter is 10 percent smaller than 700C rims, they make a stronger, better triangulated wheel. Hence, you don't need 48 spokes, as you do on a 700C wheel. The smaller wheels are lighter and offer less wind resistance, compared with the larger rim size with a 48-spoke pattern.

Equipment designs change often, but as of the date of this book, my favorite wheels use the Matrix ISO-C 26-inch ATB aerodynamic rims, with an outside width of about 20 mm, coupled with a 1 1/4-inch wide Specialized Fat Boy tire in the rear, and a 1-inch Turbo-S in the front. I find these tires have enough air volume that we don't get pinch cuts.

Tandem racing will probably expand greatly in the next few years. As thousands of tandems are sold each year, more race promoters will offer tandem events, and/or tandem classes in existing races. The Tandem Club of America (TCA) newsletter, *DoubleTalk*, has an event calendar which lists a number of different races. Tandem racers and tandem race promoters can find each other by joining TCA, at the address listed in the Appendix of this book.

We live in an era when tandeming, racing, and bicycling in general are getting many newcomers. While tandem racing isn't for everyone, the rider who would enjoy the thrill of competition can get no finer introduction than through tandem racing. And spectators enjoy tandem races immensely.

Alan Scholz, who wrote the "Tandem Racing" chapter, founded Burley Bike Bags (now Burley Design Cooperative) in 1970, and is now General Manager of Advanced Training Products, a specialty bike manufacturer in Eugene, Oregon. In his single bike racing days, he won a silver medal in the 1971 USCF National Championships.

11 • Blind and Disabled Stokers

One of the greatest joys of being a tandem captain is to take a person out for a fun, exciting ride. Often, it's been my pleasure to ride with people who don't ride single bikes much; the tandem leaves them awestruck.

Well, then, how about tandeming with someone who might otherwise never ride a bike at all? Many people can't ride a bike themselves, but they can sure enjoy tandeming. When you stop and think about it, the potential is there to share the joy of this sport with thousands and thousands of people.

Individuals who are blind enjoy stoking a tandem, as do those with other disabilities. This list includes people with problems which affect balance, an assortment of other nervous system or mental disabilities, or any cognitive deficit which would make it hard for a person to interact with other traffic.

One tandem stoker I know is a paraplegic; he rides on a specially-made Counterpoint tandem with hand cranks. (The Counterpoint tandem puts the stoker in front, in a recumbent position; the captain rides in the back in a conventional upright position. Other Counterpoint tandems have conventional foot cranks for the stoker.)

Society has traditionally consigned such people to sedentary lives, but fortunately, they now have a choice.

Some of these stokers are no slouches. Worldwide, the most famous display of blind stokers' prowess is in the *Ile de France de Tandems Handisport*, a multi-day stage race (held in conjunction with the *Tour de France)* with all sight-impaired stokers from many different countries. The best of the riders in that event perform at a level comparable to strong Category II riders in the U.S., racing about 100 kilometers per day over rough terrain and those famous bumpy French roads. (Of course, the ability range is wide. Some blind tandemists are no faster than your humble author.)

In the next few years, the opportunities for people who are blind to ride tandems will expand greatly. Tandem racing has become a top priority of the United States Association for Blind Athletes (USABA—a competition-oriented federation that belongs to the United States Olympic Committee). The USABA has found a high level of interest in cycling among its members, and it is expanding its system of training camps, coaching, and regional and national competition. At the 1992 Paralympics in Barcelona, Spain some 4,000 disabled athletes from 70 countries competed in five disability groups. Proof positive, for anyone who still needs it, that people with disabilities are serious about athletics.

Thus, it's a great time for blind athletes to discover cycling, whether for competition or for recreation; and it's a great time for tandem captains to share the sport with some very appreciative new stokers.

Tandem racers weave their way through rural France in the Ile de France de Tandems Handisport.

12 • Preventive Maintenance

It's always a drag to get out on a ride and find that your bike has a mechanical problem. Even if the problem doesn't relegate you to the sag wagon, it requires extra attention, perhaps slowing you down or cramping your style.

Don't make your riding partner a captive audience to that kind of problem on your tandem. Get everything right before you start.

The "preflight inspection" of a tandem takes only a few minutes:

- Above all else, check the tire pressure. Measure it with an accurate gauge—a tandem can't limp along with low pressure the way a single can. If the bike hasn't been pumped up in the past week, you can count on adding air pressure. Don't overinflate, but use as much pressure as the tire is rated for. Any less air pressure leaves you vulnerable to pinch cuts.
- Attempt to wiggle all racks, bottle cages, toe clips, and other accessories whose mounting screws might have loosened.

- Make sure your derailleurs and chain are adjusted, lubricated, and free of excess dirt. It only takes an extra minute to grab a rag and a container of liquid lubricant and quickly go over the drivetrain components.
- Squeeze both brake levers and check for brake adjustment. Also make sure the pads meet the rims squarely, the pads are tightly fastened to the brake calipers, the brake levers are tightly attached to the handlebars, and the cables and pivots are well lubricated.
- Make sure the timing chain is snug, and tighten the front bottom bracket eccentric if you need to. See Chapter 14 on how to do this.
- Make sure the headset bearings are adjusted properly. To do this, lift up on the handlebars about three inches and let go, so the front wheel lands on the ground. If the wheel shudders, it's a sign that the headset bearings need to be tightened.
- Your tool kit and pump should be firmly anchored in their respective places. If you have any doubts about the pump clip, use electrical tape to hold the pump in position. (I've found

electrical tape to be quite effective, holding a not-so-secure pump in place on a mountain bike in severe riding conditions. And the tape can be re-used several times.)

• Spin each wheel and make sure it's true.

• The quick-release units for the front and rear wheels should be tight, secure, and properly positioned. The cam lever must be in the locked position. (If you aren't absolutely sure how to operate a quick-release lever, get a qualified mechanic to explain it to you before you trust yourself to touch one.)

Some inspections should be performed less often, perhaps twice a season for weekend tandemists, or three or four times for mega-mileage riders:

• Inspect all cables for fraying where they meet the pinch bolts at the derailleur or brake. Sometimes one strand will break off at that point, weakening the cable. When it does, don't wait for more strands to break. Go ahead and replace the cable. Also inspect each cable where it is anchored into the cable end, inside the brake lever; any fraying there is reason for immediate replacement.

• Make sure that the fixing bolts which hold the cotterless cranks onto the crank spindle are tight. Also check the fixing bolts which hold the chainrings onto the crank spider.

• Look for cracks in your toe clips or pedals.

• Make sure the seats are securely tightened in their clamps and positioned properly for the riders.

• Check your hub brake (if you have one) for proper adjustment.

• Check the tightness of every mounting nut with an appropriate wrench. (This is a more thorough version of seeing if a rack or cage feels loose.)

These inspections are the majority of your tandem maintenance tasks. Performed properly, they'll alert you to small problems before they become big problems.

☆ ☆ ☆

A tandem may carry a heavier load than a single, but in other ways, it lives an easy life.

Usually, it's a fair-weather friend, avoiding the mud and snow that confront commuting bikes, racers' early-season training bikes, and stream-crossing single mountain bikes. So the wear and tear associated with these kinds of bike-eating elements is often reduced.

Nonetheless, you'll find when doing your annual or periodic maintenance some items may be susceptible to accelerated wear and tear if conditions are less than ideal. Here are a few to watch for:

- Crank spindles and their bearings are under greater load—particularly the rear spindle. Unless you have a sealed, lubed-for-life unit (as found on high-end tandems), have the bearings disassembled and repacked with grease if you suspect water or dirt may have gotten inside. Dirt, when combined with the higher loading of tandem use, will greatly shorten the spindle's life.
- The headset needs to be kept in good adjustment, and, like the crank bearings, repacked if the grease is dirty.
- Ditto for hubs.

- Ditto for pedals. Note that the pedals are threaded like your single bike: left-hand (reverse) on the left, and right-hand (standard) on the right. Normally both the crank arm and the pedal are marked with an *L* or *R*. In the unlikely case that you have a tandem pieced together from single bike parts, be careful—left and right threads could be anywhere.

A few components wear out more quickly on tandems than on single bikes. It's a false economy to try to stretch them past their useful life. Here are some you can expect to replace more often:

- Tires. They get more load, and the sidewalls squirm more under the higher loads. But good tires will still last well over 1,000 miles if you keep them pumped up, avoid skidding, and rotate them occasionally.
- Headset. Again, much more load, sometimes on the same bearings used on singles. (Newer tandems often have oversized headsets which are more durable.) A good quality headset, if adjusted and serviced properly, will last 3,000 to 5,000 miles. Neglected, it might go out in 1,000 miles.

• The front derailleur. Unless it's the latest indexed model, your front derailleur will spend more time scraping against the chain, because it's harder for the captain to hear that noise. So eventually you'll saw through the chain cage. Select a derailleur with a sturdy steel cage, unless you like replacing it often. Incidentally, the rear derailleur shouldn't wear any faster than that of a single bike, since it runs on the slack side of the chain.

• The drive chain. It works hard, and will stretch to the point where shifting deteriorates and it puts greater wear and tear on the chainrings and cogs.

• The chainrings and freewheel cogs, like the chain, work hard and wear eventually. (But with proper lubrication and prompt replacement of chains, these components will last much longer.)

• The freewheel body and its internal ratchet mechanism are stressed much harder. Racers and tourists alike can break cheap freewheels. So only use the best freewheel your bike shop can offer. Generally it will have two wide pawls which engage simultaneously. When you spin it in your hand, a freewheel with double-engaged pawls will have approximately 16 clicks per rotation. Freewheels best left to your single bike have their two pawls separately engaging,

Tandem specific rear hubs are available for both cassette sprockets (left) and thread-on freewheels (right). Both types shown here are threaded on the left side for a hub brake.

and those freewheels make 30 or more clicks per rotation.

A note on servicing freewheels: Almost all freewheels and drum brakes use interchangeable threads, but if you ever swap these components, you should double check. Three different thread standards—English, Japanese (ISO), and Italian—are in common circulation; they are close enough to be interchanged without damaging the components. (All use 24 threads per inch; the English uses a diameter of 1.370 inch; the ISO, 1.375; the Italian, 1.378.) Avoid parts with French threads (34.7mm x 1mm), which are not interchangeable with the others and will ruin your hub. Fortunately, these parts are no longer common. Use anti-seize compound during installation to prevent damaging hub threads at the time of removal. Tandems with a super-low gear can really torque freewheels on tight.

Instead of a thread-on freewheel, some tandems use a rear cassette hub, meaning the ratchet mechanism is incorporated into the hub itself. This allows the hub bearings on the sprocket side to be moved outboard, which provides better support for the axle. But beware! A cassette hub designed for a single bike may self-destruct when used on a tandem, and a blown-up cassette is more difficult to replace than a freewheel. So if your tandem is equipped with a cassette hub, make sure it's specifically designed for tandem use—some good indicators are a left-side thread or spline for installing a hub brake and 140mm dropout spacing.

☆ ☆ ☆

On rare occasions, you may need to perform an on-the-road adjustment. Be prepared and it won't be a big problem.

Carry a bigger tool kit than you would on a single bike. Why? The person you would probably call for a ride home is already with you. If you're stranded, s/he is too!

Your "bigger" tool kit doesn't need to be heavy or cumbersome. Mine fits in a reasonably compact seat bag—but its extra ingredients have come in handy. There was the time that a dying crank spindle bearing cartridge waited until we were 25 miles from home, late in the afternoon, to fail. I readjusted the front bottom bracket eccentric to tighten the now-loose timing chain, and we rode home without any problem.

Of course, you'll have a spare inner tube, patch kit (don't forget the talcum powder to dry-lube your inner tube), tire levers, and Allen wrenches to fit every hex fitting on the bike. That usually means 3, 4, 5, and 6mm. Check, though. Some bikes also require 2.5mm, 7mm, 1/4 inch, and who knows what. And you may also need odd-size Allen wrenches for the cleat adjustment on your shoes.

The extra tools I urge you to carry are: tire pressure gauge, chain tool, bottom bracket lock ring spanner (if applicable to your tandem), bottom bracket pin spanner, small purse-size lubricant, pocket knife, Channelock pliers, six-inch adjustable wrench, needle-nose pliers with cable cutter, spoke wrench, freewheel remover (if applicable), a rag, a cotterless crank remover/tightener, and several of those wonderful hand wipes.

A small pair of Channelock arc-joint pliers is a superior substitute for conventional pliers.

They're much more versatile, since they open wider. They can even grasp a headset locknut.

Bring a spare chain link and spare cables for derailleur and brake.

I keep some money (both change and bills) in my tool kit. You can buy lunch to pass the time if there's a delay. And I keep an old, expired driver's license, so I have an ID card that our car-crazed culture will accept.

Remember what I said about fitting all your tools in a small seat bag? All the tools and parts listed above fit in the space of two or three ordinary sandwiches. My tool bag is full, but it's small, and it's excellent insurance against being stranded.

13 • Hub Brakes

Most tandems are sold with two rim brakes and no hub brake. That's fine for most of us, but if you descend long, steep mountain passes with lots of weight, your brakes will heat up dramatically. (Tandem designer Angel Rodriguez has conducted tests that show rim temperatures of over 300 degrees in extreme conditions.) At these higher temperatures, your tires, inner tubes, and protective rim strip all soften. That's why tandem makers offer hub brakes for riders who do this kind of riding. The hub brakes get just as hot as rim brakes, but they don't take the tires with them.

Hub brakes come in two flavors: disc and drum. Some readers may need a quick review of the difference between a drum and disc brake. A drum has two internally expanding brake shoes, whereas a disc has a caliper with two brake pads that clamp against a rotating disc.

Of course, standard rim brakes are basically disc brakes which use your rim as a huge disc (several times larger than a typical disc). As a result, rim brakes have more available leverage and can use lightweight brake calipers while still providing adequate stopping power. Disc brakes must generate more mechanical advantage in the caliper itself to compensate for the smaller size of the disc. This explains why disc (and drum) brakes are generally heavier and more expensive than rim brakes.

Most of the tandem hub brakes you'll see are Arai drum brakes. Look long enough and you'll also see the elegant, expensive Phil Wood disc brake, a few old Shimano disc brakes, France's Maxicar drum brake, or the newer Hope Technology disc brake.

Hub brakes are fairly expensive, mostly because they're a rare specialty item. And with the possible exception of high quality disc brakes, their stopping power is not as good as that of a cantilever brake. But they aren't intended to stop the bike. They're intended to control your speed on long descents—a job which, because it may last several minutes, creates much more waste heat than stopping.

Because captains have only two hands, you need some ingenuity to control the third brake. Far and away my personal favorite is to attach the hub brake to a third shift lever (either thumb shifter or bar-end). On my own tandem, I control the derailleurs with bar-end levers, and a single thumb shifter controls the hub brake. The thumb shifter (it's an old pre-index model) is positioned on the handlebar tops, out of the way of my customary hand positions, and also leaving room for a handlebar bag.

The reason I like using the shift lever to control a brake is that I can dial in how much slowing force I want on a long hill, and I don't have to touch the hub brake control after that. (I can always make minor corrections by using the rim brake hand levers, if need be.)

There are several other reasons that I prefer the thumb shifter scheme: It maintains the standard brake lever configuration of the rim brakes, so tandemists who also ride single bikes will have an easier and safer transition back and forth. Because rim brakes are more powerful than the drum brake, the separate brake levers

provide better braking power for routine and emergency stops, and they reduce hand fatigue on long rides. For touring, or even around town, the thumb shifter makes it easy to use the hub brake as a parking brake.

The thumb shifter routine is very convenient, and it works better than any other scheme—and I've tried them all. (Our tandem used to have a brake lever on the stoker's handlebars, but that requires a "verbal link"—spoken commands to brake or stop braking. The verbal link is much too time consuming.)

Many tandemists control their third brake by having two cables sprout from one brake lever. I detest this approach. You have two ways of doing it, and each has drawbacks:

You can put both rim brakes on one lever, and the hub brake on the other lever. With this arrangement, you lose the ability to brake the front wheel differently from the rear wheel—and I might consider that a real loss if I were taking a fast corner and found some unexpected sand on the road. Moreover, you need more grip strength to squeeze both brakes with one hand—

Tandem hub brakes mount on the rear hub, and are great for scrubbing off speed on long descents without overheating your rims. Pictured is the Hope Technology disc brake.

something that won't be a problem most of the time, but at the end of a long day when your hands are tired, it might. One small advantage offered by this arrangement, however, is that both brakes will wear in so they are tightened an equal amount, thus slightly simplifying maintenance for you.

Your other choice is to put the front brake on its hand lever, and both rear brakes on the other hand lever. But the lever travel required for full braking is different for cantilevers and hub brakes, and you won't get full braking power. If you're willing to pay close and regular attention to adjustment, the one clever thing you can do is set the rear brake lever so the hub brake engages first, and the rim brake comes on much later in the cycle of squeezing the hand lever. When you do that, you can get a little use of the hub brake all by itself, and you still have front/rear differential braking.

Another disadvantage of the single brake lever controlling two different brakes is that replacement cables may be hard to locate, whereas the thumb shifter scheme can be ser viced by most any bicycle store you encounter. Plus, if your tandem is equipped with hydraulic rim brakes, the double cable system is simply not a possibility.

I still say the best setup is to use the extra shift lever.

If you have the ubiquitous Arai drum brake, you'll need to feed it and care for it. It has an expander mechanism with shoes that wear, just like any other brakes, and it needs adjustment accordingly. If you have an adjuster barrel on the brake cable, it is just like adjuster barrels on rim brakes and is the only adjustment the Arai drum has (other than reclamping the cable). The shoes should last you many years, since you don't use them very much.

You may need to remove the Arai drum for hub maintenance or spoke replacement. To do so,

• Remove the wheel from the bike, and remove the cable from the drum brake.

• Unscrew the axle locknut that holds the brake shoe plate on the axle.

• Remove the brake shoe plate and shoes. What's left is the one-piece aluminum casting. It's screwed onto the hub, the same way a freewheel body is screwed onto a hub.

Now you have three different ways to remove the drum:

Method one: Reach into your handy toolbox for a deep 41mm socket wrench. (You do have one in that size, right?) A 1 5/8 inch socket will also work, but it's a sloppy fit. If you use a standard-depth socket you'll probably need to remove the axle. The socket fits over the hex wrench flats inside the brake-drum casting. Secure the socket in a bench vise (preferably by holding a T-wrench or some such tool in the vise jaws), so that the socket faces up. Lower the wheel onto the socket, grab the rim, and turn the rim counterclockwise.

Method two: The aluminum casting has four 5/8 inch holes in it. Use them. Get two 5/8 inch bolts and secure them in your bench vise.

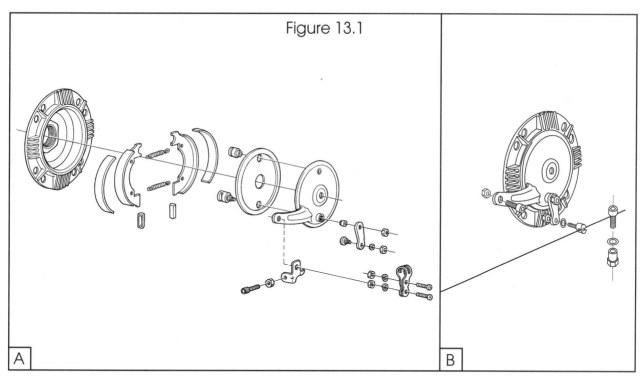

Figure 13.1

A

B

The exploded parts drawing (A) shows the inner workings of the Arai drum brake and stock cable-mounting hardware. The quick-release cable and frame mount (B) is a popular upgrade.

Position them so you can engage them in two of the casting holes across from each other, with the axle directly in between the two holes you select. Engage the casting in the holes, grab the rim, and twist counterclockwise.

Method three: This one's for desperate tandemists, stuck on the side of the road in urgent need of a drum removal, with no chance of using method one or two. Get a hammer or equivalent and a short block of wood like a two-by-four. Position the block of wood on the outside edge of the drum (against the base of one of the fins, if necessary). While your partner holds the wheel securely, tap the block of wood so it spins the drum counterclockwise. You may break a fin or crack the drum if you hit the fin anywhere other than at its base, or if the drum's on tight, so save this method for emergencies.

The hub brake threads are almost always 1.370 inch x 24 threads per inch. For reinstallation, clean the threads and, as with freewheels, always use anti-seize compound to prevent damage at the time of subsequent removal.

14 • Bottom Brackets and Chains

Adjusting the front bottom bracket eccentric (for proper timing chain tension) is easy. You should always do that job at home, as part of your periodic inspection/maintenance program, but you should also bring the tools to do it on the road, in case of emergencies.

Generally, the chain will require a slight adjustment every few hundred miles. A good rule of thumb is to adjust a new chain after about 200 miles, and readjust it every 500 miles or so after that. The consequences of a loose timing chain are dangerous! In an extreme case, the chain can come loose and fling madly. But a more insidious (and no less dangerous) risk is that when the chain is only slightly loose, it can whip sideways enough to tangle with a crankarm. When that happens, your feet are abruptly stopped. If you're sprinting at 100 rpm when that happens, it can throw you right off balance.

The eccentric should be adjusted so that when you push on the chain, midway between the two chainrings, it deflects only 1/2 inch (see Figure 14.1). (No chainrings are perfectly round; seek out their "high spot" where the chain is tightest for this test.) Do not try to tighten the chain more than this; it needs this little bit of slack to accommodate frame flex.

To adjust the eccentric, first you loosen the clamps that hold it tight in the bottom bracket

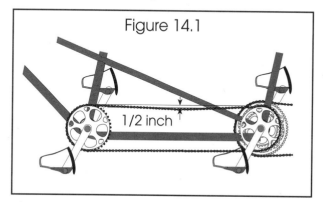

Figure 14.1

1/2 inch

The properly adjusted timing chain should deflect about 1/2 inch when pressed firmly at the center.

An eccentric with a split bottom-bracket shell employs two Allen-head pinch bolts (like a seatpost binder).

This eccentric has two Allen-head set screws that thread into the bottom bracket shell.

An internal wedge-type expander (like a handlebar stem) is built into this eccentric.

shell. These clamps come in various forms, including pinch bolts, set screws, or internal expanders (see photos at left).

After you loosen the clamps, the eccentric will still be impossible to turn by hand. The best solution is to use a bottom bracket pin tool, which engages spanner holes in the face of the eccentric. Put the tool in the holes, and use the tool as a handle to rotate the eccentric. Most tandemists rotate the bottom bracket spindle through the lower half of the eccentric shell, which allows you to sit lower on the bike. You'll rotate the eccentric about 10 or 20 degrees to adjust the chain tension, then tighten the clamps. Check the chain tension with your thumb (it may change when the clamps are tightened); if it's okay, you're done.

My tandem doesn't leave home without its pin tool. The tool is small, cheap, and lightweight (two ounces). I've only used it on the road once, but it was such a memorable occasion that I don't ever plan to leave it behind.

In this imperfect world, though, someone may need to do an on-the-road repair without the pin tool. That's why God invented screwdrivers, nails, and roadside rocks to pound with. If you find yourself without a pin tool try this: Put something like a nail or snug-fitting Allen wrench into one of the eccentric's pin holes, insert a screwdriver between the nail and the bottom bracket spindle, and rotate the screwdriver (see Figure 14.2). To prevent damage to the pin hole, make sure the screwdriver is tight against the eccentric, and don't force it.

✯ ✯ ✯

Most tandems built today use what's called a crossover drive: the timing chain which connects front and rear cranks is on the left. The drive chain which, like all drive chains, is on the right, connects the rear crankset to the rear wheel (see Figure 14.3).

Every other possible way of connecting pedals to wheels has been tried. Some put both the timing and the drive chains on the right side. This design usually limits your shifting options to two chainrings, rather than the preferred three. Its advantages are: (1) it puts much lower stresses on the rear crank spindle than conven-

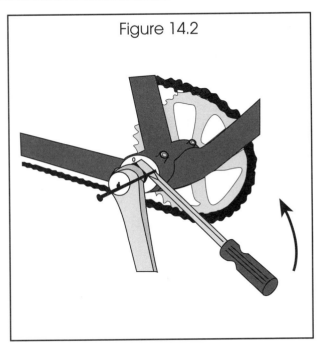

Figure 14.2

Normally the bottom bracket eccentric is adjusted using a pin tool, but in an emergency a screwdriver and nail can be used—pushing against the spindle as you twist.

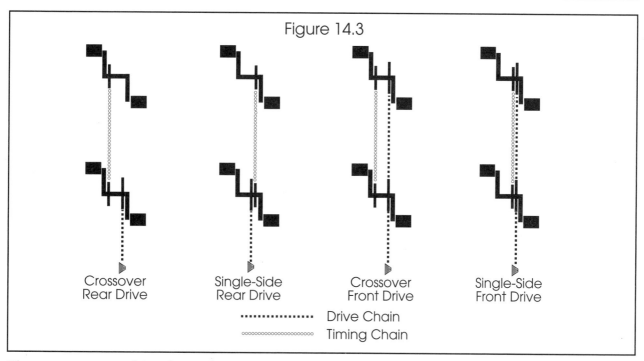

Figure 14.3

Crossover
Rear Drive

Single-Side
Rear Drive

Crossover
Front Drive

Single-Side
Front Drive

••••••••••• Drive Chain
ooooooooooooooooooo Timing Chain

The crossover rear-drive design has proven to be the favorite among most tandem builders. A single-side rear drivetrain can be built from standard (non-tandem) bike cranksets, making this a suitable setup for both entry level and racing tandems. Front-drive designs are rarely found on modern tandems.

tional crossover drive, and (2) unlike a crossover drive, it can be made from single bike drivetrain components.

Some put the timing chain on the left side, but run the drive chain from the front crankset, rather than the rear crankset. This scheme has such a long chain run that it adds nearly a pound of chain to the bike's weight. It, too, puts lower stress on the crank spindles. But that big, heavy chain can flop around a lot, so it's not a popular option.

Crank Phasing

Nine out of ten tandems you see have the cranks in-phase. The captain's pedals and the stoker's pedals are in the same position.

I vastly prefer the less conventional setup—cranks out-of-phase (see Figure 14.4). Because I occasionally have strong opinions that aren't universally shared, take note that out-of-phase cranks may or may not meet your needs.

The biggest advantage out-of-phase boosters usually mention is that they "now have a four-cylinder engine instead of a two-cylinder

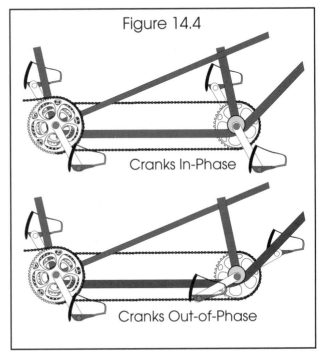

Figure 14.4

Cranks In-Phase

Cranks Out-of-Phase

Most tandem cranks are in-phase, but some tandemists prefer the handling and increased component life that come with out-of-phase cranks.

engine." There's always a rider in the midst of a power stroke.

There's another advantage which I believe is greater. It makes steering less fatiguing for the captain, and also lets the captain steer more precisely.

Let me explain: Any bike, single or tandem, has a slight tendency to weave down the road. As you push down on the left pedal, the bike wants to veer to the right. Sure, you're a good rider and you minimize that tendency. But a tandem has two people pushing on that pedal, so even with two smooth riders an in-phase tandem tends to weave. The captain has to combat that, and it requires work on his or her part to do so.

An out-of-phase tandem has none of that tendency. Even with all the different tandem partners I've had, I've never felt the bike want to weave down the road. Steering the bike becomes much, much easier.

With out-of-phase you can also expect longer life from your rear bottom bracket, rear chain, freewheel, and rear wheel, because the stresses on those components are more evenly dispersed.

Disadvantages? Riding with both riders standing takes more skill on the part of the captain. Sprinting, particularly sprinting up hills, is more difficult. (But smoothly powering up long hills is easier, thanks to the four-cylinder effect. My best tandem hill-climbing moments have been out-of-phase.) Off-road riding out-of-phase can be treacherous because ground clearance changes quickly and often, and you'll need extra concentration to keep from catching a pedal. If you still have oval chainrings you'll have to leave them off. And if you're self-conscious, be warned: you may look funny to others as you ride by out-of-phase.

People unfamiliar with out-of-phase tandems may wonder about pedaling clearance around corners. But it's a small issue. The tandem is set up so the captain's cranks lead the stoker's cranks by 90 degrees. When entering a corner, the captain points his or her inboard foot straight forward. The stoker's inside foot is up, which gives the stoker confidence, and full cornering clearance is preserved. (If the captain lifts his or her inboard foot—a very common practice when riding single bikes—the stoker's pedals will be horizontal, preserving clearance.)

You'll note that most tandem builders picture their tandems with cranks in-phase, and sell them that way. That's because most customers expect in-phase cranks. They feel more like what cyclists are used to; and techniques for starts, corners, and stops are very similar to single bike riding.

Nonetheless, I want you to get the most from your bike. If out-of-phase riding sounds like it's for you, try it! Spend five minutes with a chain tool to put the front crank 90 degrees ahead of the rear crank. Religiously use the procedure for starting and stopping I described earlier in Chapter 4; it's especially vital for out-of-phase riding. Tell the captain to go into corners with his or her inside foot forward. And enjoy your nice smooth ride.

15 • Safety

What makes tandeming safe? For the most part, it's the same things that make single bike riding safe. There are a few aspects unique to tandems, though. I'd like to cover those, and give you a refresher on the things that make all bike riding safe.

Here are the items unique to tandems:

I have one recommendation for nighttime riding on a tandem: Don't do it. I've done it myself, fortunately without ill effects, but felt it was stretching the safety margin too thin. (This, by the way, comes from a guy who is an avid nighttime rider on his single bike.)

Why no night riding on a tandem? Part of night riding is rolling with the punches. When your bike stumbles over a pebble you didn't see, you just keep going. But on a tandem, which is bigger, heavier, less maneuverable, and less spontaneous, an unexpected little bump can be frightening and perhaps hazardous. Also, a properly attentive captain will simply want to see better than you can at night, even with good bike lights. And riding at night can be unnerving for the stoker.

(If you insist on ignoring this advice, let us remind you that every nighttime rider needs bright lights front and rear. Pick safe, wide roads with little traffic. I also would implore you to have a second taillight to aid other road users in determining your position and speed, and to serve as a redundant safety backup, in case your primary light burns out. Use reflectors and reflective clothing as adjuncts. But the best advice is to save all that stuff for your single bike.)

Another difference between tandems and singles, day or night, is that on a tandem, it's more difficult to use last-minute body English to bail yourself out of a jam.

For example, if you ride your single bike into a corner too fast and start to skid sideways on some sand you didn't bother to look for, you can go through all sorts of gyrations to make it through the corner in one piece. But on a tandem, the stoker's weight makes it much harder to muscle the bike around.

Besides, if you value the stoker's peace of mind, you aren't going to want to pull stunts like that.

Therefore, plan ahead! Watch the road ahead and don't take risks.

A tandem should be maintained to higher standards than a single bike. On a tandem, it's more difficult to compensate for all sorts of mechanical imperfections. For example: Suppose the limit screws on your rear derailleur are a bit out of adjustment. On a single bike, you might go ahead and ride the bike, and just remind yourself to be careful when shifting to the innermost cogs—not the most prudent possible course, but something that people sometimes do anyway on a single. But on a tandem, that would court disaster.

Why? On a single, it's easier to detect a misadjustment through the sound of the derailleur and the feel of the pedals, and monitor that feel to avoid shifting the chain into the spokes (or recover the chain even after it's started to go into the spokes). On a tandem, the derailleur is two feet farther from you, so you can't hear it as well. Another person's feet are on the pedals, so it's harder to detect drivetrain problems through the chain.

There are other examples: Out-of-true wheels or wheels with loose spokes can magnify their problems under the heavier loads of a tandem. Under-inflated tires—my pet peeve, so easily prevented—will cause you pinch cuts if you're lucky, or worse if you're unlucky. Poorly adjusted brakes or brake cables in need of lubrication won't give you the stopping power or fine control you need with your 400-pound vehicle. There are other examples, but the central point is this: keep your tandem in excellent condition.

By the way, I've never found this to be a time-consuming or bothersome requirement. If my tandem has been inactive for some time, I spend 15 minutes pumping the tires and making sure everything is tight and properly adjusted before embarking on a ride. See Chapter 12 for my inspection checklists.

A tandem captain needs to be alert. Sure, you can ride when you're tired, but when you reach the point where fatigue cuts into your judgment, or your arms and hands feel leaden, get off the bike and take a break. Have your stoker give you a back rub to rejuvenate you before you resume riding.

Those of you who ride a mountain tandem, take note: A mountain tandem can't do everything a mountain single can. Chapter 9 on mountain tandeming goes into this in more detail, and most of the limitations aren't truly safety-related. (Rather, they involve the ignominy of having to get off the bike and walk.)

But some people will manage to make the capability limitations of a mountain tandem into safety problems. They're the kinds of people who think high-speed descending on rough logging roads on a mountain tandem is comparable to descending on a single bike. It isn't. Unless you've got traction, the tandem will want to keep going straight, twice as much as the single.

If you've ever watched a rider on a single mountain bike start to lose control at high speed and then recover, flailing wildly as he leaves a plume of dust in the air, you'll shudder at the thought of trying to do that on a tandem. Besides, the environmental impact of the tandem's plume of dust would be greater.

Captain fatigue is especially important in mountain bike riding, because steering the bike takes more work. There are all these rocks to dodge.

Make sure your tandem—or any bike you ride—is set up with the front brake hooked up to the hand lever you're used to. If you borrow or lend a bicycle, make sure the brake cables are hooked up for the rider. Left/front is standard in the U.S., but a few bikes are set up the opposite way. Even a highly skilled rider cannot reverse his or her "handedness" in the split second of a panic stop.

You'll probably ride your tandem in a group a fair amount. Do so with respect and caution. Will you draft other riders? Drafting other bicycles on a tandem requires greater skill than on a single, and it also requires excellent coordination and non-verbal communication between captain and stoker. When you get a bit too close to the lead bike and need to let up on the pedals, the stoker must sense this and let up as the captain lets up. You may find this stressful, at least at first. And if either rider simply doesn't like drafting, you shouldn't do it.

Any group of riders can tend to clog the road, which can annoy other road users and induce them to attempt unsafe passing maneuvers. Make sure your group doesn't do that; a group of tandems can be a bigger problem than a group of singles. It takes longer for a group of tandems to spread out to allow someone to pass than it takes for a group of single bikes, so you need more group coordination and forethought.

Any group of riders can tend to get carried away with the fun of the ride. When that happens, you'll see some riders act carelessly, forgetting there's other traffic on the road. Don't allow that. If you have to play policeman and lecture people, go ahead—you may be doing them a huge favor.

☆ ☆ ☆

Whether you're riding your tandem or a single bike, anticipate possible pitfalls or road hazards.

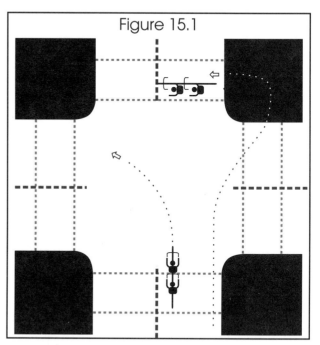

Figure 15.1

There are two ways to make a left turn: (1) Like an auto. Signal, move into the left lane, and turn left. (2) Like a pedestrian. Ride straight to the far-side crosswalk. Walk your bike across.

If you have to cross train tracks or a lip from low pavement to higher pavement, do so at a slow speed, and at a perpendicular angle. Many accidents are caused when people try to cross these lips at a shallow angle. The lip steers the front wheel out from underneath the bike.

Of course, it's possible to get a wheel caught in a sewer grate. Steer clear of sewer grates whenever possible—even if they don't catch your wheel, they are slipperier than the road surface. Start your sewer-grate-avoiding maneuver far ahead of time, so you have time to look behind for overtaking traffic; then signal and merge as necessary.

A tandem captain may find it more difficult to look behind than s/he does on a single bike. (And even if you find it easy to look, your view of traffic may be blocked by your stoker, sitting there with binoculars and having a grand time.) You may want to use a rearview mirror on your tandem, even if you don't use one on your single bike.

Make your intentions obvious to other road users. Of course this includes signaling turns (covered below), but that's not the only instance.

For example, you let people know you're proceeding straight and not turning simply by keeping your speed up and riding in a straight path. Think about the signals given off by your bike's motions, your facial expression, and your posture on the bike—and use those signals to your advantage.

When you make a left turn, do it the safe way! If traffic isn't too severe, a captain with good riding skills can look behind for overtaking traffic, and when there's a space, signal and merge to the left lane (or left side of the single lane). Wait for oncoming traffic to clear, then complete the turn. Your stoker can watch for traffic and help signal the turns. You have to be proficient at starting and stopping the tandem to make this kind of left turn comfortably, because you may have to stop for a minute while waiting for oncoming traffic.

If you're still acquiring the skills to perform this kind of left turn, or if traffic is too severe, don't try to merge into it. Ride straight through the intersection to the far curb, dismount, reposition the bike, and ride off in the new direction, or walk across as shown in Figure 15.1.

Think ahead to what the other guy might do wrong. As you approach an interaction with another vehicle, always be ready for that vehicle to do something unexpected.

Is it signaling a turn? Watch for "body English" to confirm that it will turn.

Did it stop at a stop sign, and did the driver look at you? Don't assume the driver actually saw you.

The list goes on, but the principle is simple: Think of the mistakes other people might make. Where appropriate, test their intentions by signaling and see if they respond to your signal. Be on guard for those mistakes, use a wave of the hand or a cheerful (but loud) "Hello!" as a reminder, and know what you'll do if the other person insists on carrying out the mistake.

Because you're a sophisticated bicyclist, you already know that you shouldn't do all that stuff you were warned about as a kid. But I have to mention it anyway. Don't run traffic lights, ride on the wrong side of the road, hang onto motor vehicles, pass on the right in a motorist's blind spot, carry a third person on your tandem's handlebars, or any of that stuff. Okay?

Obeying traffic laws can be summed up in two principles: (1) show common courtesy to other road users, and (2) wait your turn. Everyone else has to. You have virtually all the rights and responsibilities of any other vehicle in all 50 U.S. states and most other countries (with some exceptions like freeway access). Enjoy those wonderful rights!

Good judgment on the part of the rider is the most important safety item. No book can anticipate every situation you might encounter while riding. Never stop using your head.

And last but not least: Wear a helmet! Anyone can have a fall. If you're wearing a helmet, you'll probably be able to hop right back on the bike and keep going. If you land on an unhelmeted head, you could be in for major misery.

Virtually all helmets now sold in the U.S. offer good crash protection, because they meet the high technical standards of the American National Standards Institute. They have a sticker that says so; the sticker reads ANSI Z90.4. Most helmets also meet the somewhat higher standards of the Snell Memorial Foundation and have Snell certification stickers. (Snell stickers add several dollars to the retail price of a helmet, which pays for the organization's certification and field testing.)

Other testing standards are starting to appear in helmets sold in the U.S. The standards of the American Society for Testing and Materials (ASTM) are roughly similar to Snell's. You may also see helmets tested to the national standards of Canada, Australia, New Zealand, England, or a proposed uniform European standard. All of these standards, despite their fine-print differences, mandate a reasonable level of injury protection.

Many riders I've met sincerely believe that they don't need helmets because they ride carefully, they don't race, and they think ahead to avoid crashes. They are wrong. Anyone can fall. Even a slow-speed fall can be deadly if you land on your head. It will probably be harmless if you land on your helmet.

I can't place too much emphasis upon the importance of helmets and safe cycling habits when tandeming. A great tandem ride is always a safe tandem ride.

Appendix

Bikecentennial

Membership is $22/yr. (Canada $30/yr.) For information about Bikecentennial contact:

> Bikecentennial
> P.O. Box 8308
> Missoula, MT 59807
> (406) 721-1776

Duet Cycling Classic

For information about the Duet Cycling Classic tandem stage race contact:

> Duet Cycling Classic
> 4080 Stewart Road
> Eugene, OR 97402
> (503) 687-1644

League of American Wheelmen

Membership $25/yr. For information about the League of American Wheelmen contact:

> League of American Wheelmen
> 190 W. Ostend St., Suite 120
> Baltimore, MD 21230
> (410) 539-3399

Tandem Club of America (TCA)

Dues are $10/yr. (Canada $13/yr., other international $16/yr.) For information about the Tandem Club of America and their newsletter, *DoubleTalk*, contact:

> Tandem Club of America
> Malcolm Boyd & Judy Allison
> TCA Treasurers
> 35 E. Centennial Dr.
> Medford, NJ 08055

United States Association of Blind Athletes (USABA)

For information about the United States Association of Blind Athletes (USABA) contact Charlie Huebner or Peter Paulding at:

USABA
33 N. Institute
Colorado Springs, CO 80903
(719) 630-0422

United States Cycling Federation (USCF)

For information about the United States Cycling Federation contact:

USCF
1750 East Boulder Street
Colorado Springs, CO 80909
(719) 578-4581

Index

About the Author ...

John Schubert, a bicycling writer since 1975, and tandemist since 1980, is technical editor of *BikeReport*, the Bikecentennial member magazine, and author of the Ballantine book *Cycling for Fitness.* An accomplished bicycle tourist and self-described second-rate bike racer, he has published hundreds of bicycling articles in 14 different magazines and has been quoted in publications on four continents. Among his published articles have been road tests of several dozen tandems. Schubert also wrote the book *Running,* published by Fodor's Sports. When he isn't cycling or running he enjoys dogsledding, aerobatic flying, and searching for the perfect glass of ale.